Dear Joe,

Hope you enjoy this book,

With warmest wishes

[signature]

WHAT OTHERS ARE SAYING ABOUT SARAH THRIFT AND THIS BOOK

"An excellent guide for success. Sarah's insights and wisdom show how to translate your ideas and thinking into concrete plans and results."

– Jim Spillane, Director, *ConnectED*, Sprint

"The collaborative approach to strategy design that Sarah describes so articulately in her book is exactly what is needed to create real impact in the world."

– Zach Leverenz, CEO, EveryoneOn

"Sarah is a wonderful teacher and has transformed my ability to think strategically and communicate clearly. Whether you are reading *Designing a Strategy that Works* or attending her strategy courses, you are in for a life changing treat!"

– Janet Jenq, Internet Marketing Manager, eBay Inc

DESIGNING A STRATEGY THAT WORKS

Defining Goals
Making Choices
Delivering Results

Sarah Thrift

AVIVA
PUBLISHING
NEW YORK

Designing a Strategy that Works:
Defining Goals, Making Choices, Delivering Results

Published by:
Aviva Publishing
Lake Placid, NY
Office: (518) 523-1320
www.AvivaPubs.com

Insight Consultancy Solutions, Inc.
222 Broadway, 19th Floor, New York, NY 10001
Office: +1 (415) 413-8590
Email: info@insightconsults.com

ISBN: 978-1-943164-26-4

Library of Congress: 2015909047

Editors: Nicole Sultana (3rd edition); Irian Weber (1st and 2nd editions)
Cover Designer: Tanicia Baynes / Lollifox Design Studio
Book Layout: Nishad Shamnadh and Elambaruthi Vimal
Author Photo: Yohanna Jessup

Every attempt has been made to properly source all quotes.

Printed in Great Britain by 4edge Limited

Third Edition

4 6 8 10 12 14

To my dear friend Irian,
whose wisdom, love and patience
is an inspiration.

CONTENTS

INTRODUCTION

"Cat: Where are you going?
Alice: Which way should I go?
Cat: That depends on where you are going.
Alice: I don't know.
Cat: Then it doesn't matter which way you go."

Lewis Carroll, *Alice in Wonderland*

No organization can perform at its best unless it is working together towards the same goal. Yet research shows that only 14 percent of employees have a good understanding of their company's strategy and direction.[1]

That is if the company actually does have a strategy—35 percent of organizations don't and for their employees there is no goal to work towards. If the organization doesn't know what their goals are, then just as for Alice, it doesn't really matter which direction or choices their employees make. It's not a situation any of us want to be in, yet, sadly, it's all too common.

Perhaps you are looking to design a new strategy for your organization, your division, or for a personal project. Or maybe you have been pursuing a specific strategy for a number of years and are wondering if it's time to change course and craft a new strategy.

Maybe you recently developed a strategy but unexpected events in the market have you questioning whether your strategy is still valid.

Perhaps you have what feels like a great strategy on paper, but it never gets implemented, never produces results. Or maybe you and your colleagues put a lot of effort into aligning behind your strategy only for several colleagues to still be working and behaving exactly as before. If so you are far from alone.

Sixty-one percent of C-suite executives say their organization struggles to bridge the gap between strategy design and its day-to-day implementation.[2]

I have been there. I know how frustrating it is not to have clear direction, or to have clear direction, but for colleagues to be pulling in different directions and pursue everything but the agreed strategy. I have been on the receiving end of strategies that sound good in theory but which neither myself nor my colleagues had any idea how to implement. I don't enjoy being in these situations and I suspect neither do you.

Designing a Strategy that Works is a step-by-step guide to maximizing success in designing and implementing a strategy. It demystifies what strategy is and removes the sense of fear that can accompany the mere mention of the word.

By applying the tools, techniques and principles in this book, you will be able to shape the future of your organization. Your goals will be clear, so you can make better choices for yourself and for your organization. Your goals will be shared, so you can move forward together. You will have thought deeply about how best to deliver your goals, and the pros and cons of different options and strategies to do so. This will enable you to be much better prepared to respond to unexpected events, to quickly determine the implications and to then decide whether to stay or to change course. You will also enhance your confidence about your strategy and your ability to deliver—and that will shine through to colleagues, employees, investors and customers alike.

I have worked with hundreds of organizations all over the world, both for profit and nonprofit, designing strategies and implementing them. I have worked with Fortune 500 companies and several of the largest NGOs. I have also worked with start-ups and with small founder-led nonprofits that are doing amazing work in the developing world. I love that through this book, I have a chance to partner with you and your organization to solve entrenched problems and deliver results.

As a child, I happily spent hours solving math problems. This led me to study a Masters in Math at Imperial College, London, where I graduated with top honors and first in my class. I then combined these skills with my passion for people, working as a strategy consultant at the world's preeminent management consultancy firm, McKinsey & Company.

My experience at McKinsey & Company was very formative—my first job out of college—and gave me the amazing opportunity to learn from colleagues and clients. I used this experience as a policy advisor in the UK Treasury and before I was 30 ran a sales team of over 250 people.

I created Insight Consultancy Solutions as a way to design and deliver strategy using the very collaborative methods I developed throughout my career — a philosophy about teaching the techniques I use as a consultant so you have the skills to design your next strategy yourself.

It was back in 2008 when a client asked me if I could develop a course on strategy, he promised to bring along his CEO friends if I would write and teach the material. Since then, the demand for my course has grown and grown and I have taught the course to hundreds of executives in Fortune 500 companies, NGOs and beyond. Attendees of my courses repeatedly tell me that learning how to design a strategy changed their life. It has also changed my life—what I have learned from my course participants has made this book possible.

Whether you are part of a multinational business or a one-person organization, whether your aim is for-profit or not-for-profit, this book provides practical techniques to solve your most pressing problems and is designed as a step-by-step guide to designing a strategy that works. Use it as a reference, to be read and re-read throughout design and implementation of your strategy.

Throughout, I will be your partner for the change you want in your organization. Think of me as your coach and mentor, with you every step of the way. You don't need to do anything to get started apart from a desire to deliver your goals and a willingness to try the techniques in this book.

1

FUNDAMENTALS

*"Failure comes only when we forget our ideals
and objectives and principles."*

Jawaharlal Nehru

KEY IDEAS

Strategy derives from the Greek word "**στρατηγία**" (strategia), meaning "the General's art". Whether you are a General, run a business, work in politics or lead a nonprofit organization, your fundamental tasks in designing your strategy remain the same: determining your goal, assessing your starting point, and once both of those are clearly determined, choosing the best set of actions to take you from your starting point to your desired end point.

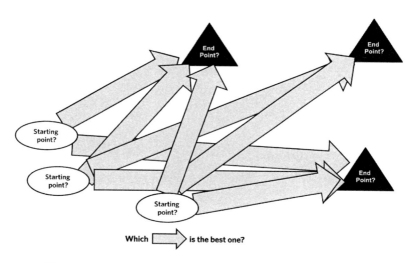

Figure 1.1: Need a clear end point and starting point to determine right actions

Identify the decision makers and key stakeholders for the strategy design process and involve them from the outset, so as to come to a shared understanding of the starting and end points. Without this shared understanding, you will never reach alignment on the set of actions to take.

Great strategy emerges from exploring a comprehensive range of options and determining which can best deliver your goal. The process of thinking through and testing various options keeps you open to possibilities and forces an explicit weighing up of the different combinations and possibilities. In essence, this is about the ability to structure thinking clearly and logically, and to translate abstract ideas into a plan that can work.

Thinking in a structured way makes you a nimble navigator. As circumstances change—and they inevitably will, with ups and downs in the market or changes in regulations—having thought through your options allows you to respond quickly, thoughtfully and competitively. You will have already evaluated the strengths and weaknesses of your options and so won't need to go back to the drawing board every time there is a change.

A strong strategy comprises a coherent set of deliverable actions that forms a bridge from your starting point to the realization of your goal. Deliverable means that if you were given any of the options to implement, all would be sufficiently tangible for you to be able to create a plan and to begin delivery.

If the strategy is conceptually brilliant but impractical or if your set of actions is vague or incomplete, then your only hope for the success of your strategy is that someone may be able to piece together something that just so happens to go in the direction you intended.

Beware of also being seduced by an elegant strategy that is a bad fit for the culture of your organization. Poorly fitting strategies are doomed to disappear in your manager's desk drawer, never to be executed.

A successful strategy is explicit about the choices underpinning it and about choices that have been rejected; or as Harvard Business School professor Michael Porter famously said, "The essence of strategy is choosing what not to do."[3] Good strategy emerges from an explicit undertaking to stop any activities that are not part of the strategy. A strategy that tries to do it all risks spreading attention and resources in all directions. Whether your organization is big or small, spreading yourself too thin carries a high failure rate.

Any great strategist, like all the great Generals of history, will put great effort into ensuring that their choices are understood by all stakeholders, be they managers, employees, suppliers or customers, and are supported by the key people who need to deliver them.

With a strategy grounded in the realism of today's starting point, designed with strong input from the people who will need to deliver it and with an objective assessment of a range of options, you will have a strategy with both the thinking and the support in place to help you overcome challenges and successfully deliver your goal.

KEY PRINCIPLES OF THE APPROACH

Actionable, Rigorous and Collaborative, or ARC for short, are the three principles that underpin my approach to strategy design and delivery. They are of such fundamental importance for any strategy process that they are introduced here, before describing the process itself.

ACTIONABLE

If you want to see your strategy implemented, it needs to be actionable—from the goal you set, to the choices you make to deliver the goal, to the implementation plan you create to deliver on these choices. For example:

- The goal is clear, stretching and sufficiently tangible for concrete actions to be determined
- Each and every component chosen as part of the strategy is actionable
- The chosen set of actions can be swiftly translated into a credible and realistic implementation plan.

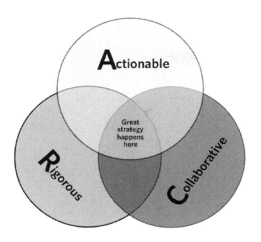

Figure 1.2: ARC - Three key principles

RIGOROUS

Despite some beliefs to the contrary, strategy is not rocket science. You don't need an MBA or a PhD or experience working as a strategy consultant. What you do need however, is a rigorous approach to both the design and delivery of the strategy.

If you are not rigorous, you risk missing out on opportunities or rubber stamping a strategy that's already in your mind. With rigor you can test what the best strategy really is. A rigorous and objective approach will also engender trust in the findings.

Examples of being rigorous include:

- Precisely wording your goal
- Being exhaustive about the range of possible choices
- Structuring your thinking so nothing important is missed
- Thoroughly exploring diverse sources of information to illuminate your decision-making
- Being transparent about your approach for assessing different options and the criteria, facts and rationale for your choices.

COLLABORATIVE

Simple as it sounds, much of the best thinking is a result of getting the right people into the right discussions. Working collaboratively with key stakeholders throughout the strategy design process is one of the most critical ingredients for success. You need the people who will be delivering the strategy to believe in it, so they can deliver well and be ongoing advocates.

To create this collective ownership, you need to identify key stakeholders from the outset and rigorously map out how to engage them throughout the process, for example by:

- Discussing and reaching alignment on the goal
- Developing a shared view and diagnosis of the starting point
- Collectively reviewing and discussing pros and cons of different options and making decisions from this shared understanding.

With this principle of collaboration I'm not advocating that you seek agreement on everything in the strategy, this risks watering everything down to the point where what is agreed isn't very meaningful. What I'm talking about is alignment. Everyone does not have to agree with everything, but everyone has been heard and is willing to align behind the decisions made.

APPLYING ARC

While each principle is important in its own right, the real magic comes from applying them together.

ARC is the backbone of my approach to all strategy design and delivery work. If you make it part of your approach, you will give yourself the right foundations for a great strategy.

You need to be just as rigorous in thinking through and setting up your framework for collaboration as you are with your evidence.

Not only do plans need to be actionable, but so too does the list of evidence to gather. Collaboration enables you to create a shared goal and to agree what level of rigor will be sufficient to make decisions.

KEY CONCEPT: SEEK ALIGNMENT

- Discussions often become challenging when each party believes they need to come to full agreement and each need to get 100 percent of what they want
- Alignment is about having a shared understanding and commitment regarding a situation and a decision that each party is prepared to support as if it were their own
- Focusing on reaching alignment rather than agreement enables a solution better than any developed in isolation. Seeking alignment means that a solution does not get stuck or watered down just because not everyone can fully agree
- Being aligned also creates the right foundation for accountability and action.

STRATEGY IN 5D

Strategy in 5D describes the five-step process I use to design and deliver a strategy that works. Its backbone is ARC and it includes tools and techniques to help structure and test your thinking, which is the heart of what you need for a robust strategy.

Steps 1 to 4 relate to the design of the strategy and address four key questions:

Step 1 - Define: What is your desired goal and end point?

Step 2 - Diagnose What is your starting point?

Step 3 - Develop: What are the viable options to take you from your starting point to your desired endpoint?

Step 4 - Decide: Which is the most appropriate set of options to deliver your goal?

Step 5 - Deliver: The final step relates to putting the strategy into practice and addresses the following key question:

Is the plan delivering and are there things you need to change to realize your goal?

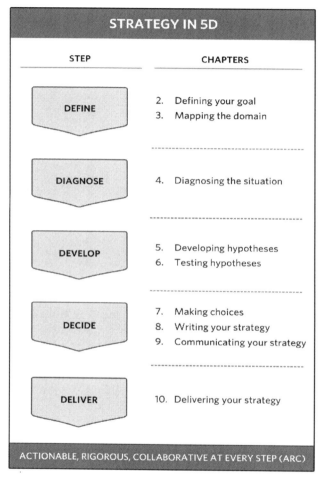

Figure 1.3: Strategy in 5D

The subsequent nine chapters of the book each relate to the steps in the Strategy in 5D process. Each chapter in the book explains in detail what is required at that particular stage of the process and includes an opening section with key ideas, followed by a table detailing the deliverables, tools, application of ARC and key meetings required. Each chapter provides worked examples using these tools and ends with a checklist.

CASE STUDY: ITC SOLUTIONS

To demonstrate the techniques, each chapter will include working examples for ITC Solutions, a fictitious IT company reselling products and providing services.

You will get to know ITC Solutions well as we apply the Strategy in 5D process to create its strategy.

ABOUT ITC SOLUTIONS

- ITC Solutions (ITC) is a technology provider with two core businesses: reselling IT products and provision of IT services
- Over the past three years it has experienced 8% revenue growth, yielding $360m in 2015
- Profitability has been flat in this same period and in 2015 was $35m
- A corporate plan estimated $42m profit for 2018, but this was rejected by the leadership team as insufficiently ambitious
- The CEO believes the next two years are critical to reinvigorating the company and kick-starting a growth trajectory and require reaching $50m profit
- Several large services contracts are up for renewal during 2016-2018
- Growth of the business has been slowed down by lack of capabilities, such as IT skills to support both internal and customer transformation.

GETTING STARTED

To get started with ARC and Strategy in 5D, I recommend the following:

1. **Appoint a strategy design leader.** This should be the person who will steer the thinking and who holds overall responsibility for the design of the strategy (steps 1 to 4 of Strategy in 5D). You will later need someone to oversee the delivery (step 5), although this may or may not be the same person.

2. **Select a strategy design team.** The strategy design leader should form a core team of people who will do the day-to-day work on the strategy design. Their role will include identifying and gathering information, drawing insights from the information, making recommendations on choices and preparing communications and presentations about the strategy.

3. **Document the Terms of Reference (TOR)** for the strategy design phase detailing the objectives, roles, stakeholders and timings. The TOR ensures that the strategy design team and stakeholders all have a clear and shared understanding of their role. Ideally the TOR is created collaboratively by the strategy design team and should include the information referred to below:

   a) **Determine objectives and approach:** this is likely to be around designing your strategy and using the tools in this book to do so.

   b) **List all decision makers and stakeholders.** Ask yourself the following three questions: Who will actually make the decisions on the choices underpinning the strategy? Who else has a stake in the outcome? Who else has important influence? A person's formal power, denoted by their role, is not necessarily the same as their informal power, so consider both as you determine which category each of your stakeholders sits in.

   c) **Create a steering committee and schedule steering committee meetings.** With your decision makers and key stakeholders you want to create a steering committee. Their role is to provide regular input into the thinking and findings and also to be part of brainstorming meetings and crucial discussions about choices. I recommend having steering committee meetings fortnightly for two hours, or if your stakeholders have time, weekly, with the understanding that until you reach the final strategy that all prior steering committee meetings are working sessions and not formal presentations.

d) **Determine length of strategy design process (steps 1 - 4):** I would recommend you allow yourself between 10 to 14 weeks to develop the strategy. In my experience, it doesn't help to take any longer. Decisions that are hard after 10 weeks are still going to be just as hard after 18 weeks. If you need to go faster, you may be able to complete the strategy design in eight weeks, but I doubt it could be done faster if you want to be sufficiently rigorous and thoughtful in gathering information and having the time to reflect on what it means.

With people's busy calendars, the time commitment can often be a concern. Ensure that all stakeholders understand that your strategy shapes your destiny, so it really pays off to invest the time to get it right.

e) **Schedule strategy design team time.** Ensure regular formal time for the team to work together, including full discussion of findings.

4. **Get buy-in from all key stakeholders,** starting with taking them through the TOR and getting their commitment to the time required of them to design an effective strategy.

An example TOR for ITC Solutions is provided overleaf.

TERMS OF REFERENCE

Objective: To develop a rigorous and actionable strategy to maximize ITC's success.

Approach: Use the tools and process from *Designing a Strategy that Works.*

Decision makers:

- Jackie Johnson, CEO
- Annette Spillars, CFO
- Jim Vaughan, COO

Key stakeholders:

- Raghu Jain, Head of Large Business
- Penny Barnes, Head of Small and Medium Business (SMB)
- Desmond Evans, Head of Product Business
- Lisa Evereau, Head of Services Business

Other stakeholders:

- All staff
- Customers
- Suppliers

Strategy design leader:

- Jim Vaughan, COO

Straegy design team:

- James Edwards, Commercial Manager
- Saffron Jones, Sales Executive, Large Business
- Jennifer Jackson, Marketing Manager, SMB
- Tyler Adams, Product Manager, Product Business
- Lydia Dyson, Services Manager, Services Business

Timeframe: 12 weeks

Strategy design team working schedule:

- Strategy design team will meet every Tuesday at 8.30am for a five-hour working session, with lunch provided. In addition, each team member is expected to devote approximately one day a week to work on the project.

Steering committee members:

- Jackie Johnson, CEO
- Annette Spillars, CFO
- Raghu Jain, Head of Large Business
- Penny Barnes, Head of SMB
- Desmond Evans, Head of Product Business
- Lisa Evereau, Head of Services Business

Steering committee role:

- Provide guidance, insight and encouragement to project team as they craft strategic direction and plan
- Supportively challenge project team to get best answer
- Reinforce importance and value of strategy design techniques as a way of working.

Steering committee schedule:

- Steering committee will meet between five and eight times, two hours per meeting except for the final presentation of three-hours.
- Meetings will take place approximately every fortnight. Strategy design team will share information, findings, and ideas for discussion and as the thinking develops will test the emerging strategic plan.

Steering committee	Agenda
Meeting 1	• Review TOR, question definition sheet and question tree.
Meeting 2	• Hear full list of hypotheses to be tested • Provide feedback on any suggested changes or additions to list of hypotheses • Provide ideas for new information to seek.
Meetings 3, 4 (and possibly 5 and 6 depending on number of hypotheses)	• Hear team's findings on first tranche of hypotheses • Provide feedback on any gaps in rigor or questions still to be answered, to confirm or disprove each hypothesis.
Meeting 5, 6 or 7	• Discuss recommended choices • If there are big strategic choices to be made, ensure full discussion • Reach alignment on the key choices, for example, the key tenets of the new strategy.
Meeting 6, 7 or 8	• Hear final presentation of strategy and high-level plan • Provide feedback for any changes and guidance on how to execute.

You are now ready to embark on your first task, determining your goal and articulating it precisely as a question. Let's get started.

2

DEFINING YOUR GOAL

"It isn't that they can't see the solution.
It is that they can't see the problem."

G.K. Chesterton

STRATEGY IN 5D

STEP	CHAPTERS
DEFINE	2. Defining your goal 3. Mapping the domain
DIAGNOSE	4. Diagnosing the situation
DEVELOP	5. Developing hypotheses 6. Testing hypotheses
DECIDE	7. Making choices 8. Writing your strategy 9. Communicating your strategy
DELIVER	10. Delivering your strategy

ACTIONABLE, RIGOROUS, COLLABORATIVE AT EVERY STEP (ARC)

KEY IDEAS

You cannot design an effective strategy—that is choose a set of actions that will be effective—if you are not clear on what these actions are supposed to achieve, that is, your goal. There cannot be any ambiguity in what your goal is.

A well-formulated goal and end point should adhere to the ARC principles introduced in Chapter 1. This means that the goal should be actionable, rigorously thought through and determined collaboratively.

Questions stimulate thinking and discovery, so it works best to express your goal as a question. Take time to try different questions that express different goals or that emphasize different aspects of a particular goal. Ensure you rigorously commit every possible question to paper, with precise wording, so none are missed, assumed—based on what you think someone has in their mind— or left ambiguous.

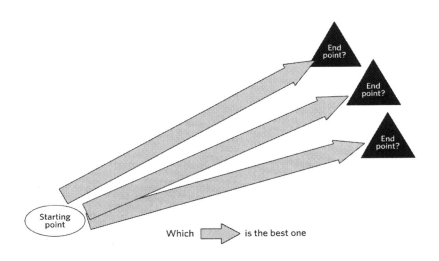

Figure 2.1: Need clear end point to determine right actions

You want your question to be stretching while remaining actionable. A straightforward and less wide-ranging question may miss important opportunities. If, however, your question is rightly straightforward then it may not require going through the full Strategy in 5D process.

Keep going until your question precisely expresses what you want. You can often feel it instinctively if this is the case. The emphasis on the right question might sound black and white and that's because it is. There is most often only one formulation that is precisely right and since your entire strategy will be developed to answer this question, you need to get it right.

As author Stephen R. Covey says, "If your ladder is not leaning against the right wall, every step you take gets you to the wrong place faster."

To check the precision of your question and to ensure buy-in, involve your stakeholders in its formulation. Don't be surprised if there are diverse views about what the question should be. Make sure everyone is heard and ideally ask an external person to facilitate the discussion, with the aim of alignment—you are not seeking 100 percent agreement—behind one question.

As I often say when teaching my strategy courses, your question shapes your destiny, so take the time to think and get it right.

DELIVERABLES, CONCEPTS, ARC AND MEETINGS

Deliverables	• Question Frame
Key concepts	• SMART ONE question • CORD to frame the question
Application of ARC	• Goal and question are stretching, yet **actionable** • Question is worded precisely and with **rigor** • Question is developed through a **collaborative** process

Key meetings	Strategy design team: • Meet to determine question and complete Question Frame (may require two meetings) Steering committee: • Review Question Frame; may also want to meet stakeholders individually prior to meeting with all.

EXPRESSING YOUR GOAL AS A QUESTION

Let's start with a few examples of goals expressed as questions to start thinking about what makes a good question. We will review questions for ITC, so you might also want to reread the "About ITC Solutions" box in Chapter 1.

Bearing in mind that your question frames the strategy developed, how appropriate are the following questions for ITC? Write down your thoughts as you read through:

1. What makes ITC profitable?

_____

_____

_____

_____

2. Can ITC double its business?

_____

_____

_____

_____

3. What organizational changes are required for ITC to double its business?

_____

_____

_____

_____

4. How can ITC add 50 percent to its revenue in the next two years, while at least maintaining current profit margins?

_____

_____

_____

5. Create a proposition to generate significant and sustainable return for ITC and the customer.

_____

_____

_____

_____

6. In what ways can ITC add 50 percent to its profitability while maintaining customer satisfaction scores?

_____

_____

_____

_____

We will return to these questions shortly.

GREAT QUESTIONS ARE SMART ONES

A great question should be a SMART ONE. You're probably familiar with the SMART acronym which defines effective objectives as being Specific, Measurable, Actionable, Realistic and Time-bound. To this, I add ONE, which stands for Open, Non-Assumptive and Expansive. Check your question to see if it is a **SMART ONE**:

Specific: Articulates your question without ambiguity. Every word matters, so be exact with your words to express your intent precisely.

Measurable: Contains components that can be used to assess sucesss, for example a profit target or a measure of social impact.

Actionable: Gives rise to concrete actions that ultimately realize the goal.

Relevant: Ensures the question gets to the heart of what is most important.

Time-bound: Provides a timeframe during which the answer to the question—the strategy—must be delivered.

Open: Cannot be answered with either yes or no.

Non-assumptive: Does not contain any implicit assumptions about the solution nor preclude possible solutions. (Ideas for potential solutions are great, just note them elsewhere).

Expansive: Has the same scope as the goal, giving space for a comprehensive range of viable options in response. Apply Einstein's advice: "Make everything as simple as possible, but not simpler."

EXERCISE: IDENTIFY WHICH QUESTIONS ARE SMART ONES?

Let's return to the the six questions for ITC. Consider how each question performs against each of the SMART ONE criteria:

Answer Yes / No	1. What makes ITC profitable?	2. Can ITC double its business?	3. What organizational changes are required for ITC to double its business?
Specific			
Measurable			
Actionable			
Relevant			
Time-bound			
Open			
Non-assumptive			
Expansive			

Answer Yes / No	4. How can ITC add 50% to its revenue in the next two years, while at least maintaining current profit margins?	5. Create a proposition to generate significant and sustainable return for ITC and the customer.	6. In what ways can ITC add 50% to its profitability while maintaining customer satisfaction scores?
Specific			
Measurable			
Actionable			
Relevant			
Time-bound			
Open			
Non-assumptive			
Expansive			

Commentary on the above table can be found in the Appendix.

THE RIGHT QUESTION: TESTING EXPANSIVENESS

A helpful way to test if your question is the right one with the appropriate level of expansiveness and really addressing the goal, is to ask: "What are the questions behind the question, and which one are you seeking to answer?"

Let's consider the following question:
   a) What changes could be made to pricing to reach $50m profitability in 2018?

A question behind this question is:
   b) What do our offerings need to be to best deliver $50m profit in 2018?

We can repeat the same step again, seeking a question behind question b):
   c) What actions can we take to deliver $50m profit in 2018?

Then decide which question provides the most appropriate scope for your strategy. To come to the conclusion that a) is the right question, you would have needed to have done prior work and already have determined that a focus on pricing will generate all viable options for reaching $50m in 2018.

Working through this for ITC to ensure the question is a SMART ONE, and knowing the context about growth having been slowed down by lack of capabilities, then a suitable question is:

"What actions can ITC best take to develop capabilities and achieve sustainable profit of at least $50m per year from 2018?"

APPROACH TO GETTING THE RIGHT QUESTION

Crafting a question that is a SMART ONE through collaboration is an excellent way to create buy-in from stakeholders. The best way to do this is to get all key stakeholders around the table, or at least on a conference call (see Key Concept: Good Meeting Practice on the following pages).

Conduct the meeting either as a brainstorm, or review a shortlist of possible questions. Make sure that everyone's views on potential overall questions are heard.

Ask somebody who's not a stakeholder to facilitate, their role is to engage everyone and ensure all views are heard impartially.

Pay attention to the specific words each person uses. Nuances are important. Seemingly small changes in wording can cause big changes in the direction the strategy takes.

Write down all suggestions and wording on a whiteboard or flipchart that all participants can see so you can compare the range of formulations.

Be open to differences of opinion and work through them. Often it is these differences that really open up the discussion and allow the question to evolve into a much better one. Subtle or less subtle differences of opinion or suggested points of focus need to be clarified if the subsequent strategy work is to be successful.

Iterate and reiterate the question until everyone is comfortable. If you get stuck, take a break and come back to it. There is really only one question that is better than any other and you can usually feel whether you have got to the right question.

By spending the time to get the question right in the first place it is extremely rare that you need to change it later. Only a significant change to the market, such as a change in regulation, could typically warrant a change of question and in all my years of consulting I cannot think of one instance where a change was needed. (Bear in mind the strategy design process is at most four months long, so changes to the question would only be ones dictated by significant changes to circumstances during that time. In Chapter 10, we look at what to do if circumstances substantially change once you have developed your strategy).

Remember, the aim is alignment. You don't need every stakeholder to agree with every word. They only need to feel sufficiently comfortable to align with it. If you aim for 100 percent agreement on every word, you risk diluting the question through too many compromises.

KEY CONCEPT: GOOD MEETING PRACTICE

For every meeting, whether it's a one-off or routine, think about what you want the outcome to be and how you can best achieve it. Not only does this help you get what you want, but participants are happier if you make good use of their time.

Prior to the meeting:

- **Desired outcomes:** write these down, including any decisions that need to be made and how you want attendees to feel as a result of the meeting

- **Clear agenda:** identify the items you want to cover and the time allocated to each. You may want to do this by consulting participants. Then circulate the agenda to all participants

- **Meeting approach:** determine the nature of the meeting. For each item will there be a question to discuss, slides presented, a brainstorm or something else?

- **Pre-read/prep:** Be sure to circulate any materials with time for attendees to read in advance. Highlight any topics or questions for thought prior to the meeting

- **Delineated roles:** Ensure you know in advance who will play what role, including whether you will have someone chairing the meetings and/or someone facilitating

During the meeting:

- **Frame the meeting:** Even if you think it's obvious, remind participants of the purpose of the meeting and the role you want them to play (provide feedback, make a decision, primarily listen). This need only take a couple of minutes and is invaluable for getting all participants to a common starting point

- **Set ground rules:** Be explicit about the behaviors required from all to ensure success. You don't need to do this every meeting, but you should do so with a new group or if an existing group has started to exhibit bad behaviors. It often works well to get participants to tell you what behaviors they see as required

- **Take minutes:** Give an attendee responsibility for writing down all the meeting points, including actions, owners and timing. This will form the basis of the meeting write-up and needs to be objective.

- **Stay on track:** Start on time and manage time so you get through the agenda; if further discussion is required set up a separate time

- **Maintain roles:** Do not deviate from roles decided for the meeting. For example if your role is to facilitate, do not start offering your views

- **Articulate clear next steps:** Wrap up each item with clear actions with owners and timing for each

- **Next meeting:** Agree next meeting as required, with date, time, location and purpose

After the meeting:

- **Circulate write-up:** include actions, owners and timing within 48 hours of meeting. To ensure accountability, start with a review of progress on these actions at the beginning of the next meeting.

CLIENT EXAMPLE: REACHING ALIGNMENT

Four stakeholders of a large multinational company working in travel and entertainment and I were sitting around a table.

One of the stakeholders described what he believed the question to be. So, we began with his question, which focused on reviewing an existing business, to ensure we had the best commercial model. It soon became apparent, however, that the other three stakeholders each had different views on what the key question was.

Another stakeholder wanted to review the whole industry and from there create the commercial model, not just for the existing business, but for all future businesses.

The stakeholders were very surprised that everyone else had such a different view on what the question was to be and a fantastic debate followed, enabling a burgeoning of ideas and building a more fitting question than any of the original four.

Through this process the stakeholders also realized they had unknowingly been holding different objectives and expectations and that a simple meeting got these resolved in the best interest of the business.

The stakeholders thanked me for helping them reach an aligned position. This hadn't been my direct objective—which was getting to the right question—but it was invaluable to get this engagement between stakeholders. This engagement continued throughout the project and beyond.

ADDING A CORD: CONTEXT AND DELIVERABLES

Once you have determined your question as a SMART ONE there are four supporting areas to add to relating to your question: the **CORD** (Context, Opportunity, Results, Deliverables), which along with your question provides your Question Frame.

QUESTION FRAME	
Question	What SMART ONE question are you seeking to answer?
Context	What background information would you need to tell someone to give them appropriate context on the question?
Opportunity	Are there any stipulations or constraints to the scope that are not articulated in the question? For example, a question only applicable to certain countries and business units
Results	Are there other results that need to be achieved beyond those explicitly articulated in the question? For example, non-financial objectives such as industry accreditations or levels of employee retention
Deliverables:	What do you want to come out of the strategy design work? For example, a written strategy document, business plan, interim milestones, resource plan, technology plan, decision rights and governance, comms plan.

Following is an example of a completed Question Frame for ITC that comprises the SMART ONE question plus the CORD:

QUESTION FRAME	
Question	What actions can ITC best take to develop capabilities and achieve sustainable profit of at least $50m per year from 2018?
Context	• ITC is a technology provider with two core businesses: reselling of IT products and provision of IT services • Over the past three years, has experienced 8% revenue growth, yielding $360m in 2015. • Profitability has been flat in this same period and in 2015 was $35m • A corporate plan estimated $42m profit for 2018, but this was rejected by the leadership team as insufficiently ambitious • The CEO believes the next two years are critical to reinvigorating the company and kick-starting a growth trajectory and require reaching $50m profit • Several large services contracts are up for renewal during 2016–2018 • Lack of capability in the business has slowed down growth. For example IT skills to support both internal and client transformation
Opportunity	• All business divisions, North America and Europe • Would consider geographical markets beyond this as part of growth strategy

Results	• Profit in 2016 and 2017 needs to be at least $42m and $45m respectively • Establishment of a learning culture that encourages the testing of new initiatives and the ability to learn fast what works well and what does not

Deliverables	• A clear set of actions, that will be executed to deliver the strategy, including:
	
	  - Revenue and number of new customers as well as profit targets
	
	  - Description of new markets and new services provided and how to win new business in these
	
	  - The resources and capabilities that will be needed
	
	  - Governance of these actions including assigned owners for each set of actions or deliverables and a review approach to determine success quickly
	
	  - Quarterly milestones for 2016, six-monthly for 2017 and 2018
	
	• Recommendations on creating a learning culture
	
	• Identification of risks and countermeasures
	
	• Communications approach to engage all members of business with this strategy

Figure 2.2: Example Question Frame for ITC

You can use the Question Frame along side your Terms of Reference to provide details of the process, your stakeholders and the question.

Review both documents at least once a week throughout the first four stages of Strategy in 5D to avoid going off track. It is all too easy to get lost in the weeds, so bring yourself back up to bird's eye by reviewing your original intentions with the question and in so doing ensure that you come up with a robust strategy in service of your question.

QUESTION CHECKLIST

- The question is a SMART ONE
- The question is written down
- Key stakeholders have been engaged in developing or reviewing the question
- Key stakeholders are in alignment with the question
- The Question Frame has been completed
- Key stakeholders are aligned on the Question Frame, including each aspect of the CORD.

3

MAPPING THE DOMAIN

"Do not worry if you have built your castles in the air. They are where they should be. Now put the foundations under them."

Henry David Thoreau

STRATEGY IN 5D

STEP	CHAPTERS
DEFINE	2. Defining your goal 3. Mapping the domain
DIAGNOSE	4. Diagnosing the situation
DEVELOP	5. Developing hypotheses 6. Testing hypotheses
DECIDE	7. Making choices 8. Writing your strategy 9. Communicating your strategy
DELIVER	10. Delivering your strategy

ACTIONABLE, RIGOROUS, COLLABORATIVE AT EVERY STEP (ARC)

KEY IDEAS

With your question defined, your next step is to identify sub-questions, that is, the questions you need in order to answer the overall question. By breaking down the overall question into sub-questions, you create structure: a map of the domain filled with the questions you need to answer in order to address the overall question.

Compare this for a moment with trying to directly answer the overall question without putting any further structure in place: it's a bit like starting an essay without having thought through any structure for your argument. It's hard to assess where best to start and it's all too easy to forget to include key points. Similarly here, if you go straight to answering the overall question, there is a significant risk of missing potential solutions.

Identifying all possible sub-questions opens up new perspectives and may lead to surprising and profound insights that will in turn lead to unexpected solutions and a better strategy. Even if you have a hunch that a particular sub-question will not lead to a viable solution, still include it. Now is not the time to restrict thinking but to embrace all possibilities.

To avoid overlap, you want the sub-questions to either be completely distinct from one another or to be sub-questions to a sub-question, i.e. they break the sub-question down to the next level. This ensures you won't miss out on a potential line of investigation.

It helps to organize your sub-questions visually into a question tree as depicted in Figure 3.1. The question tree positions sub-questions relative to each other based on their content. Sub-questions become more detailed as you move to the right. The first tier of sub-questions are not too detailed and together they answer the overall question to their left. The next tier of questions to the right, tier two, are the sub-questions to the tier one sub-questions, and so on. As such, the tree creates structure between the sub-questions by making the relationship between them explicit.

You want as many tiers to your tree as required, but also for the sub-questions of the final tier to be of a manageable scope such

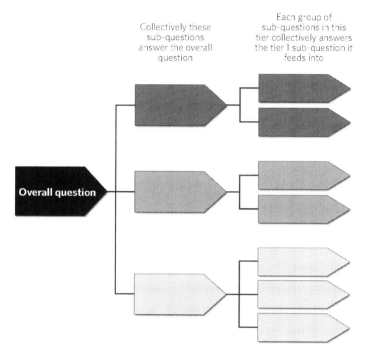

Figure 3.1: Question tree structure

that they can be thoroughly addressed. In most instances I find that two tiers of sub-questions are sufficient.

Some sub-questions may be answered directly with facts, such as with most sub-questions relating to the past and present. Other sub-questions, such as those relating to future or potential opportunities cannot be answered by facts alone and will need to be answered with a combination of evidence, such as a combination of customer feedback and insights from experts. Such sub-questions can best be addressed through first generating hypotheses of the most plausible answers. Then, using the evidence gathered, each hypothesis can be tested, revised and ultimately confirmed or rejected. We will return to this in much greater depth in Chapters 5 and 6.

As with every step of the strategy design process, be sure to get alignment from your key stakeholders. This means getting buy-in for your question tree. That way, you can be sure that the map of the domain it provides does not miss anything important. You also safeguard against stakeholders coming back at a later stage and asking why a certain question or set of questions were not considered.

DELIVERABLES, CONCEPTS, ARC AND MEETINGS

Deliverables	• Question tree
Key concepts	• Sub-questions • MECE (Mutually Exclusive, Collectively Exhaustive)
Application of ARC	• Sub-questions are **actionable**: either they can be answered as is, or are broken down into further sub-questions, until each is answerable as is • Sub-questions are generated with **rigor** to ensure that nothing is missed • Key stakeholders review and align with the question tree and where possible, are also engaged **collaboratively** in the generation of sub-questions
Key meetings	Strategy design team: • Brainstorm sub-questions and then organize into a question tree Steering committee: • Review question tree and make any changes until reach alignment on the tree.

EXAMPLE SUB-QUESTIONS

Sub-questions break open the overall question into logical and more manageable components. You can break down all sorts of questions—not just strategy ones. One of my colleagues at McKinsey used to map out a question tree to determine options for her Friday night out!

Most sub-questions begin with either "what" or "how" and need to be formulated as a question, not a statement. Every sub-question needs to be complete in and of itself—although it may still require further breaking down to a level where it can be practically analyzed or researched.

We talked earlier about the overall question being right. There is no one right set of sub-questions, although you can have a wrong set if there are gaps or overlaps. To check for this, you need to ensure that if you were to answer all the sub-questions, you would have an answer to the overall question without the need to answer any further sub-questions.

Let's take a couple of examples:

Example 1: What is the most time- and cost- efficient way to get from New York City to Washington D.C. leaving tomorrow morning and arriving by 2pm?

Sub-questions could be:

1.1   What are all the ways to get from New York City tomorrow morning to Washington D.C. by 2pm?

1.2   How much does each of these cost?

1.3   How much time does each of these take?

1.4   Given the above and the overall question, what is the best travel option?

Example 2: In the next 12 months, how can Generate, a youth nonprofit, increase impact for its current users without increasing costs?

Sub-questions here could be:

2.1   How does Generate define and measure impact today?

2.2   Is this sufficient for their needs or do they need to further develop this and if so, what would this look like?

2.3   What levers do Generate have to increase impact without increasing overall costs?

2.4   How easy are the levers to implement and show results within the next 12 months?

2.5   Given the above questions, what actions should Generate take and what is the plan to do this?

Sub-questions can be generated at different levels of detail. For example, some sub-questions to sub-question 1.1 could be:

1.1.1   Which airlines fly from New York City to Washington D.C. tomorrow morning that arrive by 2pm?

1.1.2   What are the flight times?

1.1.3   Which of these flights have remaining seats?

While sub-questions can feed into another sub-question, no sub-question should directly overlap another sub-question. This means that unless it adds something new, it should be eliminated.

Let's suppose that for example 1, we also asked the following tier one sub-question:

1.5   What are the cheapest options of traveling between New York City and Washington D.C. tomorrow morning by 2pm?

Review this sub-question alongside sub-questions 1.1 to 1.4. Does it overlap?

Yes. It overlaps with sub-questions 1.1 and 1.2.

Does it add anything new? No. We should therefore eliminate 1.5 and use 1.1 and 1.2, or replace 1.1 and 1.2 with 1.5 to ensure the sub-questions remain mutually exclusive.

Let's return to questions 1.1.1 to 1.1.3. Do these overlap with questions 1.1 to 1.4? Yes, they overlap with question 1.1. Do they add anything? Yes, since they provide structure to what needs to be considered when answering sub-question 1. Which means unlike question 1.5, we don't want to just delete them. We will need them later when we structure our questions into a question tree.

APPROACH TO GENERATING SUB-QUESTIONS

A great approach to generating your sub-questions is for the strategy design team to brainstorm them. If you have stakeholders who are willing to roll up their sleeves, then involve them in the brainstorm too.

It works well to ask attendees to think in advance what the sub-questions could be. If you are facilitating the meeting, you may want to brainstorm your own list of sub-questions prior to the meeting—and be ready to check against these towards the end of the meeting once everyone has had the opportunity to share their sub-questions.

Don't limit your thinking too early. The only way to make sure you generate all relevant sub-questions is to first come up with all possible questions you might want to answer in service of answering your overall question. So allow space for the seemingly irrelevant ones, the best solutions can often come from the places we least expect.

A good approach is to ask everyone to write their sub-questions on large Post-it® notes. That way everybody can share their sub-questions by placing them on whiteboards or walls, and later when structuring the sub-questions into a question tree, you can easily move them around.

I highly recommend you read each of your sub-questions aloud, as this brings additional clarification and crystallization, beyond what can be achieved by just sounding them out in your head. It often leads to a refinement of the of the wording of each sub-question and stimulates new sub-questions.

Check that the questions are not closed (yes/no) and are articulated in a way that allows a range of possible solutions and does not lead to a particular answer to the exclusion of others.

Make your sub-questions as concise as possible without losing meaning. Be sure that they are all expressed as questions, not thoughts, ramblings or answers.

There is also no limit to the number of sub-questions. Just make sure that as well as more high-level sub-questions, you also have sub-questions that are not too big to be addressed as is.

Don't despair if you find yourself in a sea of sub-questions that seems overwhelming, having a lot of sub-questions is in fact a good sign that you are not missing anything.

What is ITC's current and historical financial performance?

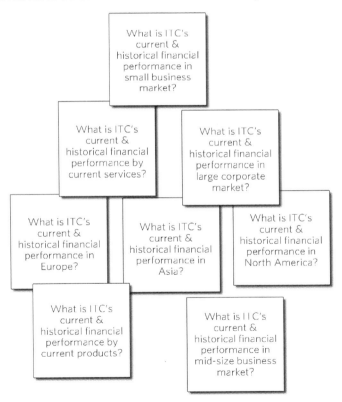

Figure 3.2: Example Post-it® notes from sub-question brainstorm

When you feel that you have most of the sub-questions, begin grouping them by topic. There is no single way to group sub-questions, often the grouping that makes most sense is the one that is in line with how information is available.

For example, you might group sub-questions about the internal situation and performance of the organization together, or put those about customer needs together, or those about regulation together. If there is a blurring of lines between topics then this will lead to research being repeated or missed.

You may need to make a choice between different groups to avoid overlaps, especially as you look at more detailed sub-questions. For example, if you have sub-questions about financial performance, one way to group these might be around geographies, that is financial performance in the different geographies today and if your scope permits, the potential financial performance in new geographies. Another way could be by customer segment, for example, grouping the sub-questions by customer size (large, medium, small business and consumer). A further way could be to group performance sub-questions by current products and services.

You typically need to chose between these groupings to avoid overlap of sub-questions, so ask yourself which will be the easiest cut to answer.

Check also that each sub-question is not in effect a rephrasing of another sub-question. Delete any direct repeats but do not remove sub-questions that are a legitimate sub-question of another sub-question, as per the example questions relating to travel from New York City to D.C. earlier in this chapter.

Check for gaps either in topics or in the sub-question grouped under a certain topic. What is missing? What else would you need to know to bring insight to this topic? Test to see that the sub-questions you have would allow for all viable hypotheses and solutions related to the topic.

Then step back and ask: taken together, would these sub-questions answer the overall question? That is, are the sub-questions collectively exhaustive, with no gaps.

What is ITC's current and historical financial performance?

What is ITC's current & historical financial performance by current services?	What is ITC's current & historical financial performance in small business market?	What is ITC's current & historical financial performance in Europe?
What is IIC's current & historical financial performance by current products?	What is ITC's current & historical financial performance in large corporate market?	What is IIC's current & historical financial performance in Asia?
Products & Services Grouping	What is ITC's current & historical financial performance in mid-size business market?	What is ITC's current & historical financial performance in North America?
	Customer Segment Grouping	**Geographical Grouping**

Figure 3.3: Grouping in sub-question brainstorm

STRUCTURING YOUR QUESTIONS: THE QUESTION TREE

Now that you have a set of sub-questions you have grouped by topic, it's time to structure them into an integrated system: the question tree.

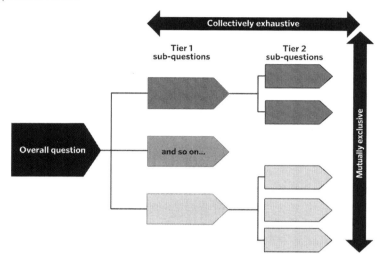

Figure 3.4: Structure of a question tree

Many consulting organizations use question trees to structure thinking and conduct analytical problem solving. This was certainly the case when I worked at McKinsey & Co. At the outset of each new project we used the process of creating the question tree as a way to open up the problem at hand and to create structure for the work to be done.

Building a tree is about finding ways to group your sub-questions logically, by topic. As you move to the right of your tree your sub-questions become more detailed. This means that within a topic area, you also want to organize your questions into different levels of detail, with those of the same level of detail sitting within the same vertical tier.

In each tier you typically want between two and eight questions. Without at least two sub-questions, you have not broken anything down. If you have more than eight sub-questions it gets hard to manage and you will usually find that the sub-questions are not all of same level and so fit more comfortably on different tiers.

Within a tier, you order the sub-questions based on the order in which you would seek to answer them, acknowledging that some sub-questions will be answered in parallel and some require that you answer other sub-questions first before they can be addressed.

For every tier of your question tree, the sub-questions of that tier need to be mutually exclusive, so no overlaps, and when taken together, they must comprehensively address the question that feeds into the next tier, that is they are collectively exhaustive.

With no gaps and no overlaps, this makes your tree Mutually Exclusive and Collectively Exhaustive, a principle also referred to as MECE.

KEY CONCEPT: MECE

MECE, pronounced "me see", is a grouping principle where information is arranged by separating a set of items into subsets that are mutually exclusive and collectively exhaustive.

- No gaps to ensure all factors are considered

- No overlaps to ensure all key questions are separated

A MECE approach helps encompass both the big picture and smaller details and this is one of the reasons why it is invaluable for strategic problem solving.

Figure 3.5: MECE – Mutually Exclusive, Collectively Exhaustive

EXAMPLE QUESTION TREES

Let's return to example 1: What is the most time and cost efficient way to get from New York City to Washington D.C. leaving tomorrow morning and arriving by 2pm?

We could translate questions 1 and 1.1 to 1.4 into a simple question tree (i.e. one tier):

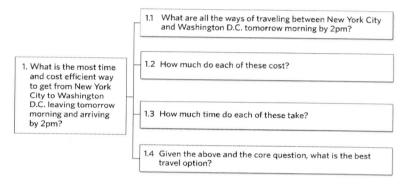

Figure 3.6: Question 1, Example Tree

Or we could take example 2 and similarly translate into a question tree.

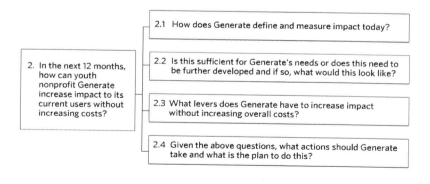

Figure 3.7: Question 2, Example Tree

Now let's take a new question, question 3: How can Roberts Ltd sustainably increase profit per annum by $100k by 2017?

A classic tree structure for a question about increasing profitability is organized around opportunities to increase revenue and/or to reduce costs.

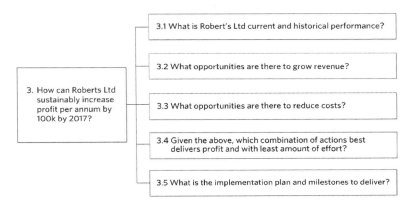

Figure 3.8: Question 3, Example Tree A

In the example above, the two sub-questions on revenue and costs (questions 3.2 and 3.3) are couched between questions to understand the context and current situation (question 3.1) and the implementation to deliver these (questions 3.4 and 3.5).

The same question 3 could also be translated into a tree organized into sub-questions around customer needs, market dynamics and competitors.

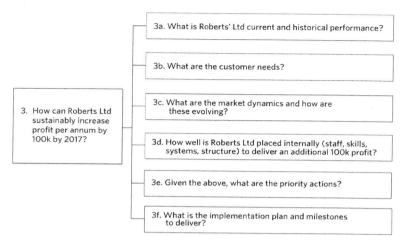

Figure 3.9: Question 3, Example Tree B

Remember, there is no right tree, but there are some wrong ones, where the tree is not MECE.

It is worth testing the number of tiers of sub-questions required for your tree. This tends to be no fewer than two tiers and is determined by whether the sub-questions are of a manageable scope or whether they need to be broken down into smaller components to better organize the work to be done.

For example, in the tree in Figure 3.10, take sub-question 3.2: What opportunities are there to grow revenue? This is unlikely to be of manageable scope to answer directly. One way to break it down would be to add sub-questions exploring opportunities to increase price, or to increase volume.

Mapping the Domain

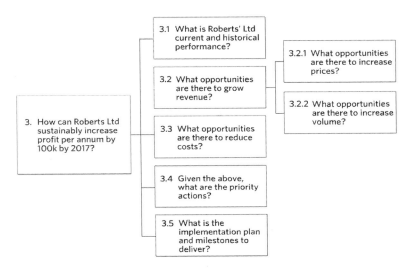

Figure 3.10: Question 3, Example Tree A with two tiers, v.1

Alternatively, question 3.2 could also be broken down into growing revenue both from existing customers and new customers:

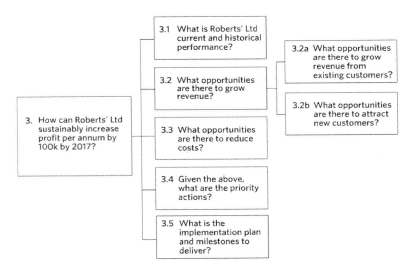

Figure 3.11: Question 3, Example Tree A with two tiers, v.2

Often, you may start to build your tree in one way, then as it develops, you might reshuffle the groupings. In some cases, questions that were in tier 2 or 3 may become tier 1 sub-questions, and vice versa. You may also add or rewrite questions to ensure the tree is completely MECE.

If you have written your sub-questions on Post-it® notes, then you can gather together the strategy design team and move the questions around on a wall or whiteboard where everyone can see them and comment on the different structures.

Don't be afraid to take a break and come back to the tree with a fresh perspective. It matters to get it right since it maps out the domain of the possible solution and the work to be done. When the structure and organization of the tree works, teams often report that the sense of a *click* takes place. Once this happens and the tree is complete, just like your overall question, bar exceptional circumstances, it should not change.

You can document your full tree visually, just as you have it drawn on your whiteboard or flipchart, or you can translate it to grouped lists of questions, written out as per the example for ITC at the end of this chapter.

Since it can get fiddly to visually document all the tiers of the tree on paper I like to depict tier one of my tree as a tree and then write out tiers two onwards as a grouped list, as shown at the end of this chapter. Sometimes, I will also add the topic of the question groupings and begin a document that I call the *Discovery Document* where I put the Question Frame followed by the tree. Excerpts of this *Discovery Document* are contained in this and subsequent chapters.

STRATEGY IN 5D QUESTION TREE STRUCTURE

Earlier I mentioned that there is never just one way to structure a question tree. That said, I often find that for strategy questions a helpful grouping of questions is that which mirrors steps 2, 3, 4 and 5 of Strategy in 5D: diagnosis (diagnose), options (develop), choices (decide), implementation (deliver). I call this the Strategy in 5D question tree grouping:

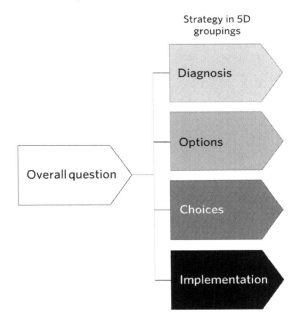

Figure 3.12: Strategy in 5D question tree grouping

Each topic typically comprises one, two or three tier one sub-questions. These sub-questions then lead to further sub-questions in tier two.

The diagnosis allows you to diagnose your starting point and the customer, industry and competitor trends that are emerging. It may often be crafted into one question about the internal situation and one on the external situation.

Sub-questions in tier two on the internal situation may include an understanding of the current mission, vision, strategy and values of the organization, its current and historical performance and its skills, capabilities, technology and processes. You also want to include any projections for the future, for example knowledge of forthcoming opportunities or of existing contracts up for renewal.

The sub-questions supporting the external situation may include regulation, economic growth, demographics, and political stability. Again, you want to include anything known or projected for the future, for example a known or expected change in regulation or trends in customer needs and the expected implications of these.

The options grouping of sub-questions can draw on the diagnosis findings and must enable exploration of all viable options to answer the overall question. The choices sub-questions may include determining the criteria you will use to select the set of options that become your strategy.

Finally, the implementation sub-questions consider what it will take to deliver. This includes staff, skills, processes, technology, investments plus the delivery milestones.

EXAMPLE TREE FOR ITC SOLUTIONS

Below is an example tree up to tier 1 for ITC, with questions shaded to identify which topic they align with in the form of the Strategy in 5D question tree grouping.

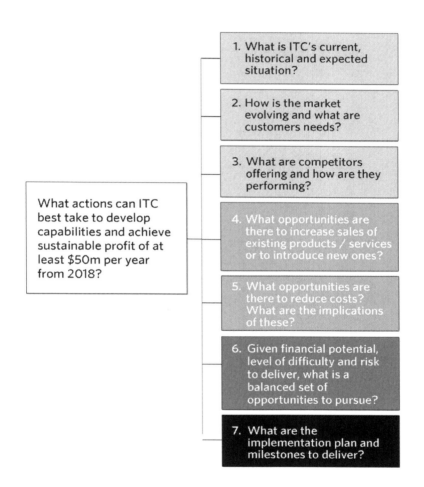

Figure 3.13: Question tree for ITC, Tier 1

Also included below is a full tree for ITC written out as text, with tier one and two sub-questions. You can add this to your growing *Discovery Document*, after the Question Frame.

ITC QUESTION TREE

DIAGNOSIS: CURRENT SITUATION

1. What is ITC's, current, historical and expected situation?

   1.1   What is our stated mission, vision and strategy?

   1.2   What is our current and historical financial performance?

   1.3   What is our organizational structure and key operations?

   1.4   What are known facts about the future? (e.g., contracts up for renewal, office leases expiring?)

   1.5   What can we expect or see possible in the future, if we assume continuing as we are today?

DIAGNOSIS: CUSTOMER NEEDS

2. How is the market evolving and what are the customers' needs?

   2.1   What customer needs are we currently fulfilling?

   2.2   Are there other customer needs we know about or could foresee?

   2.3   What is the market size, trends and projected growth?

   2.4   Are there known or possible changes in regulation?

DIAGNOSIS: CUSTOMERS

3. What are competitors offering and how are they performing?

   3.1   Who are our competitors?

   3.2   What is their current and historical performance or what are their stated projections or growth plans?

   3.3   What products/services do they offer, what are the features, pricing and what do we know about future offerings?

OPTIONS: REVENUE

4. What opportunities are there to increase sales of existing products and services or to introduce new products or services?

   4.1 What opportunities are there to provide more of the current products and services to existing customers and what could this deliver financially?

   4.2 Who and where are the most promising new customers to whom we could sell current products and services and what could this deliver financially?

   4.3 What new products or services could we provide to meet the needs of existing customers and what could this deliver financially?

   4.4 What new products or services could we provide to meet the needs of new customers and what could this deliver financially?

OPTIONS: COST

5. What opportunities are there to reduce costs and what might be the implications of this?

   5.1 What opportunities are there to reduce costs in sales and marketing and what would be the overall impact of this?

   5.2 What opportunities are there to redesign products to reduce costs and what would be the overall impact of this?

   5.3 In what ways could services be redesigned to reduce costs and what would be the overall impact of this?

CHOICES

6. Given financial potential, level of difficulty and risk to deliver, what is a balanced set of opportunities to pursue?

   6.1 What is the financial potential of each opportunity?

   6.2 How difficult is each to deliver?

   6.3 What is the level of risk and how can this be mitigated?

6.4 Are certain opportunities dependent on others?

6.5 When combined, which opportunities go well together and which do not?

IMPLEMENTATION

7. What are the implementation plan and milestones to deliver?

7.1 What implications are there for products and services offered and the need for modification to these?

7.2 Are there implications for how ITC serves their current target customers?

7.3 What is required in terms of skills and capabilities and how will these be achieved from today?

7.4 What is required in terms of processes and technology to support this?

7.5 What level of investment is required and when?

7.6 How will ITC test if the strategy is working (e.g. pilots, milestones) and how will we adapt our strategy and tactics based on what we learn?

7.7 What is the best governance to ensure successful implementation and how can ITC divide the work and assign responsibilities?

7.8 What are the internal and external communications plans?

THE TREE THAT BLOSSOMS

From the multitude of questions you first gathered, you now have structure connecting all your sub-questions.

Your question tree holds the map of all possible solutions to your overall question. This will provide you and your organization with a dynamic way of working through these issues strategically, creatively and logically.

QUESTION TREE CHECKLIST

- Everything is expressed as a question and is as clear and concise as possible

- There are no more than eight questions in tier one. If there are more, then these need to be restructured into tier two or three questions

- No sub-question in any tier is a restatement of the overall question (or of any other sub-question)

- In every tier, all questions are distinct from one another, with no overlaps (mutually exclusive)

- The questions taken together cover all possible sub-questions (collectively exhaustive)

- If you were to answer all the questions in tier one, you would answer the overall question; similarly answering all the questions in tier two would answer all tier one questions, and so on...

- Key stakeholders have been involved in generating, or at least reviewing the question tree

- Key stakeholders are aligned behind the tree.

4

DIAGNOSING THE SITUATION

*"Facts are stubborn things; and whatever may be our wishes,
our inclinations, or the dictates of our passion,
they cannot alter the state of facts and evidence."*

John Adams

STRATEGY IN 5D	
STEP	**CHAPTERS**
DEFINE	2. Defining your goal 3. Mapping the domain
DIAGNOSE	4. Diagnosing the situation
DEVELOP	5. Developing hypotheses 6. Testing hypotheses
DECIDE	7. Making choices 8. Writing your strategy 9. Communicating your strategy
DELIVER	10. Delivering your strategy

ACTIONABLE, RIGOROUS, COLLABORATIVE AT EVERY STEP (ARC)

KEY IDEAS

With your Question Frame and question tree in place, you are ready to switch gears and start answering the sub-questions related to the diagnosis. By working with your stakeholders to answer these sub-questions, you can develop a shared diagnosis of the current reality, including future developments that are certain or very likely, and a map of the internal and external dynamics you are working in.

This broad diagnosis will not only help you determine a clear starting point for the work that needs to be done, but will also allow you to dig below the surface of the facts you come across and explore connections between them. The deep understanding of the current situation you gain during this phase allows you to make more informed choices later.

If you are developing a strategy for an organization you know well you may be tempted to skip this step, thinking you know what the current situation is—but do you really want to gamble the future of your organization on what you think you know? If you misdiagnose the starting point then the set of actions you choose for your strategy are unlikely to be the right ones and will not lead you to your goal.

A thorough and rigorous diagnosis requires assessing the full set of facts without bias or assumption. It also requires being open to new facts that may change your previous view of reality.

It is likely that your stakeholders will offer their view of the current situation at the beginning of a strategy process. However, never assume that your combined views comprise a complete set of information. Always double check the facts: I have lost count of the number of times I have been told information about an organization's financial performance only to later discover that this information was wrong when I looked at their financial statements.

A rigorous diagnosis also requires you to think without cognitive biases. This refers to work that has been done in decision science that demonstrates how susceptible we are to flawed and biased thinking. One such bias, confirmation bias, leads us to see what we expect to see. Which means that instead of objectively analyzing the information we gather, we instead assume it tells us what we expect.

Becoming familiar with some of the main cognitive biases humans fall prey to is the first step to avoiding them. Questioning our own thinking in this way increases our ability to objectively find and interpret information, and as a result, makes us more effective decision makers.

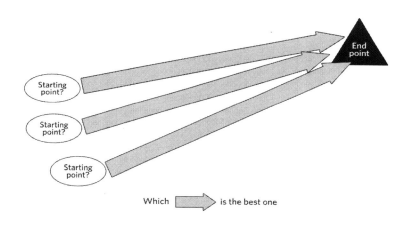

Figure 4.1: Need a clear starting point to determine the right actions

EXAMPLE: DIAGNOSING THE SITUATION

Let's say your goal is to increase profit by $2m. You know quality is very important to customers. Without gathering more facts, you assume that any reduction in cost will not be tenable, due to quality requirements, and hence make revenue your sole focus.

Your set of actions will then be about ways to increase revenue. But what if you were to gather information and discover that costs had been reduced 10% over the past three years with no impact to quality and indeed that your top 10 customers had all reported improvements in quality.

Suppose also, customer feedback showed that beyond a certain quality threshold, customers got what they needed quality-wise and didn't need—or want—to pay for any more.

Then it would be limiting to exclude reducing costs as a potential action relevant to your strategy.

If you are using the Strategy in 5D question tree grouping (from Chapter 3), then typically the first two or three sub-questions in the first tier of your tree, plus their sub-questions, provide the areas for exploration of the current situation.

It is not uncommon to uncover facts that are inconsistent and so you will need to determine what is the most accurate view and diagnosis of the situation. This may be based on the reliability of different sources or on the weight of evidence leaning in one direction more than another.

You may want or need to supplement facts with interviews, such as with staff, market experts or customers, to add richness and test inconsistencies. When you communicate your findings, ensure that you are clear what is fact and what is interview-based feedback.

You need to describe and document your diagnosis in a way that is easy to understand and that highlights what is most important, without information overload.

Your audiences need to understand the implications of what you are sharing and why it is important. Otherwise, your audiences will make their own inferences and not necessarily those you intend. This makes it your job to make clear why each piece of information is relevant and to connect the dots between seemingly disparate pieces of information.

A great way to do this is to structure your thinking using the Minto Pyramid Principle®, which groups information logically and connects the dots by linking information and drawing out implications.

Don't just jump into the diagnosis phase. At the outset, be sure to create a workplan listing information and sources with clear responsibilities and timings. In the context of your full strategy design process, the diagnosis phase should take between 25 percent and one-third of the time of the next phases of hypotheses testing. Working backwards, this typically indicates around two weeks of work.

DELIVERABLES, CONCEPTS, ARC AND MEETINGS

Deliverables	• Diagnosis information table • Diagnosis dummy deck • Diagnosis implications table • Diagnosis document • Diagnosis synthesis
Key concepts	• Cognitive biases • Dummy pack • One message per slide • SWOT • PESTLE • The Minto Pyramid Principle®
Application of ARC	• All information sought has sources identified, making the gathering of them **actionable** • Facts and evidence are researched and presented fairly and **rigorously** • Facts and evidence on the current situation are shared, with implications discussed **collaboratively**
Key meetings	Strategy design team: • Meeting 1, identification of facts and evidence to be gathered through review of question tree. Meetings 2 and 3, review of evidence and then of draft diagnosis document Steering committee: • Review diagnosis document, identify any gaps and further work to be done to complete diagnosis

IDENTIFYING THE INFORMATION YOU NEED

To identify what information you need to assemble, return to your list of sub-questions. Reread all the tier one questions that relate to the diagnosis. Then also read their sub-questions in tier two and beyond.

A good way to do this is to brainstorm the list of information, either as a team brainstorm or ask each person to make their own list on Post-it® notes and then for all to share with the group.

Below is an example for ITC, with sub-questions one to three, those that are relevant to diagnosis:

DIAGNOSIS INFORMATION TABLE	
Sub-questions	Required information
1. What is ITC's current, historical and expected situation?	
1.1 What is ITC's stated mission, vision and strategy?	• Mission Statement • Values • Written strategy (if exists)
1.2 What is ITC's current and historical financial performance?	• Profit & Loss (P&L) statement, balance sheet and cash flow past three years, split by Business Unit (BU) • Projected budget and performance this year and any future years • List of key customers by BU, revenue, profit and percentage of BU total

1.3 What is ITC's organizational structure and key operations?	• Organizational diagram including key job titles and holders
1.4 What are known facts about the future?	• Contracts up for tender with size ($) and date • Key known changes in personnel (if any) • Known IT system changes • Known ends of office leases
1.5 What can ITC expect in the future if they continue as they are today?	• Develop assumptions for future growth based on known customers, insights from historical performance and customer insights • Extrapolate financial performance for next three years
2. How is the market evolving and what are customers' needs?	
2.1 What customer needs are ITC currently fulfilling?	• Preliminary list of customer needs compiled from brainstorm and interviews with staff
2.2 Are there other customer needs ITC know about or could foresee?	• Feedback from customer surveys • Customer interviews, testing list of needs
2.3 What are market trends, current market size and projected growth?	• Definition of markets in which ITC play today, plus their size today and projections, ideally for next three years

Sub-questions	Required information
2.4 Are there known or possible changes in regulation?	• List of any known or expected changes in regulation, compiled from both team brainstorm and review online
3. What are competitors offering and how are they performing?	

3.1 Who are ITC's competitors?	• List of competitors with:
	  – offerings
	  – key customers
	  – size ($)
	  – number of employees
	  – key locations

3.2 What are competitors' current and historical performance and any stated projections or growth plans?	• Profile per competitor listing:
	  – Core products and services
	  – Key customers
	  – Revenue and profit past three years
	  – Any information on strategy and growth plans
	
	• Interview any staff who are former employees of competitors

3.3 What products and services do they offer, what are the features and pricing and what does ITC know about future offerings?	• Add key features and pricing to each competitor profile • List any information about future plans

ORGANIZING THE WORK TO BE DONE

Collation of the required information is a great opportunity for the strategy design team to start doing research work together and works best when tasks are divided among the team.

To do this effectively you want to group facts with similar sources together and then agree responsibility and timing for completion. In instances where you may need to talk to people as well as request facts, such as when identifying customer needs, then agree upfront who to talk to.

It works well if strategy design team members can choose areas of particular interest to them. This does not have to be areas they know best and in fact, given our propensity for cognitive biases, it can actually work better to gather facts in an area where you have limited knowledge. So plan to discuss who will do what and by when as part of the strategy design team meeting.

Below is an example workplan for ITC, including sources, owner and timing for each piece of information sought.

DIAGNOSIS INFORMATION TABLE AND WORKPLAN			
Sub-questions	Required information	Source	Owner & timing
1.1 What is ITC's stated mission, vision and strategy?	• Mission Statement • Values • Written strategy (if exists)	• CEO's office • Corporate Comms • CEO's office	James 14th January

Sub-questions	Required information	Source	Owner & timing
1.2 What is ITC's current and historical financial performance?	• Profit & Loss (P&L) statement, balance sheet and cash flow past three years, split by BU	• Finance team	James 18th January
	• Projected budget and performance this year and any future years	• BU Directors	
	• List of key customers by BU, revenue, profit and percentage of BU total	• BU Sales and Commercial Directors	
1.3 What is ITC's organizational structure and key operations?	• Organizational diagram including key job titles and holders	• HR team	Jennifer 14th January

Sub-questions	Required information	Source	Owner & timing
1.4 What are known facts about the future?	• Contracts up for tender with size ($) and date	• Large Business and SMB Commercial Managers	Tyler 18th January
	• Key known changes in personnel (if any)	• HR	
	• Known IT systems changes	• IT	
	• Known ends of offices leases	• Property team	
1.5 What can ITC expect in the future if they continue as they are today?	• Develop assumptions for future growth based on known customers, insights from historical performance and customer insights	• Strategy design team, based on review of information gathered in 1.1 to 1.4 and also in 2.1 and 2.2	Tyler 18th January
	• Extrapolate financial performance for next three years		

Sub-questions	Required information	Source	Owner & timing
2. How is the market evolving and what are customers' needs?			
2.1 What customer needs are ITC currently fulfilling?	• Preliminary list of customer needs compiled from brainstorm and interviews with staff	• 8+ members of staff; need to firm up list	Saffron 18th January
2.2 Are there other customer needs ITC know about or could foresee?	• Feedback from customer surveys • Customer interviews, testing list of needs	• BU Heads • At least 6 customers; need to firm up list	Saffron 21st January
2.3 What are market trends, current market size and projected growth?	• Definition of markets in which ITC play today, plus their size today and projections, ideally for next three years	• Internet • Analyst/ research firm reports	Lydia 18th January

Sub-questions	Required information	Source	Owner & timing
2.4 Are there known or possible changes in regulation?	• List of any known or expected changes in regulation, compiled from both team brainstorm and review online	• Internet • Government Department and agency websites • Industry Groups • Meeting with mix of staff (TBC who)	Jennifer 21st January
3. What are competitors offering and how are they performing?			
3.1 Who are ITC's competitors?	• List of competitors with : - Offerings - Key customers - Size ($) - Number of Employees - Key locations	• Interviews with sales staff • Competitor websites and financial accounts	Lydia 18th January

Sub-questions	Required information	Source	Owner & timing
3.2 What are competitors' current and historical performance and any stated projections or growth plans?	• Add revenue and profit past three years to each profile • Interview any staff who are former employees of competitors	• List of staff (names TBC)	James 21st January
3.3 What products and services do they offer, what are the features and pricing and what does ITC know about future offerings?	• Add key features and pricing to each competitor profile • List any information about future plans	• Competitor websites and financial accounts • Interviews with sales staff and former competitor employees	Jennifer 21st January

Determine upfront how you will document your findings. You want to make this as simple as possible while ensuring the findings will be accessible and that all sources of information are clearly cited.

If you are familiar with using slides to communicate information then ask each owner to put the core findings into a handful of slides. Later we will discuss how to make the slides really compelling, but for now it suffices to get the relevant information into slides (or whichever format you are using e.g. prose document).

Assign one member of the strategy design team to collate all the information and ask each owner to forward their material to that person for collation. You may want to mock-up your slides as part of the work done together as a team. That way you can be clearer about what you expect to get back from each owner.

This is called a dummy deck or dummy pack, and comprises the title of each slide—which is your best informed guess of the likely finding—plus a note of the information you will be providing on each slide to support your finding.

You can do this directly in PowerPoint although I find it easier to take a piece of paper and then divide the page into nine or 12 rectangles and use this as a storyboard for my dummy slides. I like to handwrite this information in pencil as this means I can easily change it, as I invariably move the order of the slides, their titles and the information to go on them.

You want to have one key message per slide—and not more. For example, suppose you know that you want to review the revenue growth over the past three years, so you will want a slide displaying this output. This ensures clarity of message. If you have more than one important message then split it onto multiple slides, one for each key message. Since you don't know what the revenue growth will be, your best approach is to assign the title: Revenue has grown by [x%] over the past three years and insert the unknown in square brackets once you have the information (see slide three overleaf).

You also want to list on the body of the slide how you will present the information. The information in square brackets explains the format, for example text, line chart, bar chart, quotes. You also want to add the owner for the slide—as has been done shaded in grey in the right hand bottom corner of the subsequent dummy slides.

Once you have reviewed the information, you may want to change the title as well as fill in any square brackets in the title. You will likely find out that some titles are completely wrong—for example it may be that revenue did not grow at all in the past three years.

It may also be that you want to highlight a more specific finding, for example: Revenue has grown at a consistent [y%] for each of the past three years, or Total revenue growth has been [z%] the past three years, masking swings between single and double digit growth.

Provided you are willing to change titles—and indeed scrap slides and/or add new ones—a dummy pack is a fantastic instrument to ensure consistent structure and a focus on the desired end product.

Example ITC dummy slides:

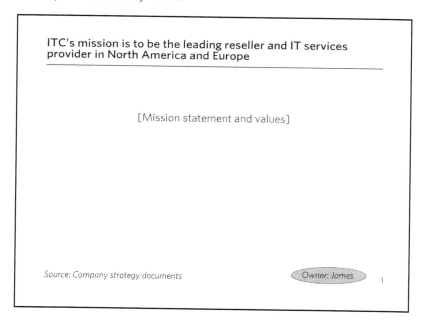

Its stated strategy, designed five years ago, focuses on being a reseller and not on services

[Key tenants of latest documented strategy]

Source: Company strategy documents

Owner: James   2

Revenue has grown by [Y%] over the past three years

[Line chart of revenue by year, with % growth by year & overall]

Source: Management accounts

Owner: James   3

This comprises [Z%] growth with medium size business and [A%] decline with large business

[Line chart of revenue growth by customer size, past three years]

Source: Management accounts   4

Profitability has grown by [B%] over the three years, with highest profits from [customer segment C]

[Line chart of profitably overall and by customer size]

Source: Management accounts Owner: James 5

Revenue and profitability are projected to each grow at [D%] and [E%] respectively per year for next two years

[Budget table or chart, showing projections]

Source: Management accounts

Owner: Tyler   6

Today [F] customers comprise [G%] of our revenue

[List of customers, revenue and profitability]

Source: BU Account lists; Management accounts

Owner: James   7

Of these [H] have contracts up for renewal in next three years

[Table of contracts up for renewal, with date and likelihood of winning or potential new contract terms]

Source: BU Account lists; Management accounts; interviews with sales staff

 Owner: Tyler

8

The business is matrix organized around sales units and product/services units

[Organizational diagram]

Source: HR

Owner: Jennifer

9

ITC's market share in the small business market—their biggest market—is only [I%]

[Table or chart of markets and size today, plus any projections]

Source: Management accounts;
Gartner report on US IT market, 2016

 Owner: Lydia   10

The key customer needs served today are [J, K,L]

[List of customer needs]

Source: Sales staff interviews; Customer survey 2015;
Customer interviews

Owner: Saffron   11

There is evidence to suggest M and N may [become needs / become bigger needs]

[Explain M and N]

Source: Sales staff interviews; Customer survey 2015; Customer interviews

 Owner: Soffron   12

There [are/are not] key regulatory changes expected over the next three years

[List of comments / quotes from web searches or interviews]

Source: Department of Commerce; Internet searches   Owner: Jennifer   13

ITC have [O] key competitors, [P] of whom are growing fast

[Table of competitors, key financials and offerings]

Source: Department of Commerce; company websites

Owner: Lydia

14

Competitors [Q] and [R] have quite [similar/different] strategies

[Details of strategies for each key competitor]

Source: Staff interviews; Company websites

Owner: Lydia

15

With your diagnosis dummy pack in place, you are now ready to gather and analyze the required information.

MITIGATING FOR COGNITIVE BIASES

As you embark on your very first phase of research, it is important for everyone in the strategy design team (and beyond) to be aware of cognitive biases. That is, assumptions and mistakes in reasoning that we unconsciously make that lead to biases in the information we seek, how we receive and assess information, and ultimately the decisions we make as a result.

Traditionally, economists believed in the human being as a rational thinker and that facts and information would be carefully weighed before decisions were taken. Decision science debunks this notion and describes many of the shortcomings of human decision-making. For example, research by Dr. Daniel Kahneman and Dr. Amos Tversky[4] found that many human decisions rely on automatic or knee-jerk reactions that are based on rules of thumb that we develop or have hard-wired into our brains .

In the book *Moneyball: The Art of Winning an Unfair Game*,[5] Michael Lewis tells the story of Oakland Athletics baseball team and how manager Billy Beane adopted an analytical, evidence-based approach to assembling a competitive baseball team. Despite Oakland Athletics having less money than other baseball teams, they were able to recruit more successfully.

The central premise is that the collective wisdom of insiders working with Oakland Athletics and other baseball teams was subjective and often flawed. Their conventional wisdom valued qualities such as speed and contact. Yet rigorous statistical analysis had demonstrated that on-base percentage and slugging percentage were better indicators of offensive success—and these qualities were cheaper to obtain. By adopting a recruitment strategy based on targeting on-base percentage and slugging percentage, Billy Beane was able to cost effectively assemble a winning team.

It's not easy to adopt a Moneyball approach. Defaults are very powerful and you may not work in an organization that has an objective, data-driven decision process, which is what enabled Oakland Athletics to identify undervalued indicators of success. Even if you do work in a data-driven culture, if the data is contrary to conventional wisdom, most people will still try not to accept it and resist changing their thinking.

What you are looking to do is to inoculate yourself against cognitive biases. This enables you to gather and assess information without bias, which in turn provides the best foundation for effective decision-making.

The following introduction of several key biases serves as an initial inoculation shot, so to speak, to allow you to be aware of and mitigate for each of them as you design your strategy.

WHAT YOU SEE IS ALL THERE IS

Daniel Kahneman coined the acronym WYSIATI, which is an abbreviation for "What you see is all there is". It captures the human tendency to passively accept the formulation given and to form impressions and judgments based on the information that is available to us or at hand rather than asking: "Is what I see all there is?", "What information am I missing?" and "What if the reverse were true?"

WYSIATI can also play out by assessing information too quickly and superficially. In his book "*Thinking Fast and Slow*"[6] Dr. Kahneman uses the following example which I invite you to answer:

"A bat and a ball together cost $1.10. The bat cost $1.00 more than the ball. How much does the ball cost?"

Take a look in the Appendix and see how you fared. If you got it wrong, you are in good company: fifty percent of Havard and Yale students got this wrong. Eighty percent of the students who were asked this question from other universities got it wrong. This is WYSIATI thinking. It is fast, easy, comfortable and lets you come up with a quick answer or decision, but one that is likely wrong.

WYSIATI can interfere when you are interviewing someone for information for your strategy. It shows in the questions you do and don't ask and how consistently you follow-up with questions on things that are raised.

As you now gather the information, ask yourself:

• What am I not asking?

• What am I not seeing?

• What information am I missing?

CONFIRMATION BIAS

Simply put, it is easy to miss something you are not looking for. Even more so if implicitly you are expecting or wanting a certain result and so are predisposed to look for this in your information.

This is the essence of confirmation bias: the tendency to look for, interpret and remember information in a way that confirms our preconceptions.

This, for example, comes into play when describing an organization's financial performance. You may have a preconception of how the organization has performed and then cite information to support this and yet this information may only give a partial and hence potentially misleading picture of financial performance.

Hence the importance of asking what is missing from the facts you have gathered and then filling in those gaps, and challenging yourself with the question "What am I not seeing?", before making any decisions.

AVAILABILITY BIAS

Availability bias is the tendency to estimate the probability of events by how easy it is to think of examples of such events. This can be influenced by how recent the memories are, for example through direct experience or through what we have read or heard in the media, or how emotionally charged they may be. Essentially, the ease with which something comes to mind is used as a proxy for how likely it is to occur.

Take the following example:

A man under 40 years of age in the US or the UK is more likely to die as a result of? Please check one:

☐ Terrorist attack

☐ Homicide

☐ Suicide

☐ Car accident

What did you respond? If you replied terrorist attack, homicide or car accident then you would be with the majority. And certainly we hear a lot in the media about all of these. But in fact—and quite tragically—suicide is a more frequent cause of death than any of these and is the most common cause of death among men under 45 in the UK.

OVERCONFIDENCE BIAS

Read through the table following and provide estimates for each of the eight items, plus a lower and upper estimate where you are 90 percent confident that the actual number lies within this range:

To estimate, all for 2015	Main Estimate	Low	High
1. GDP per capita in the US			
2. Proportion of books sold in electronic format in the US			
3. Proportion of American public school students qualifying for free or reduced school lunches			
4. Population of European Union			
5. Number of nations in the United Nations			
6. Your organization's worldwide revenue 2015			
7. Your organization's worldwide net assets, 31 December 2015			
8. Your organization's worldwide employee turnover 2015 (%)			

For how many of the eight questions do you think you provided a range within which the actual number occurred?

Now go to the Appendix and take a look.

If you are like most people, then you will have been overconfident. Alpert and Raiffa's work showed that 42.6% of quantities fell outside of participants' 90% confidence ranges.[7]

These results do not improve for questions where you are a subject-matter expert, that is, the same level of overconfidence persists[8] (or at times can be worse as experts can be more convinced that they are right).

In terms of your strategy design work, this means that whatever you do, seek full information and allow yourself to be surprised about what it is telling you.

CONTROLABILITY BIAS

If we are in control of something we tend to associate less risk with it—for example we see less risk when we are driving than when someone else is. Or we see more risk in flying versus driving where we are not the one piloting the aircraft but would be driving the car.

This could translate to business too. For example, if a key customer's contract is up for renewal, research suggests that you will be more confident about retaining it if you are in charge rather than if one of your colleagues is in charge. Yet there is no rational evidence to back this up, so beware not to implicitly make this assumption as part of your findings.

STATUS QUO BIAS

All else being equal we tend to choose the status quo option. The status quo is taken as a reference point and any change from that baseline is perceived as a loss.

This can be seen quite dramatically in an example of people signing up for organ donation by country. In Europe, there are big differences by country in the level of organ donation. In Figure 4.3 you see those countries on the left where a minority (4% to 28%) of the population participates in the organ donor program and those on the right where the majority (86% to 100%) participates.[9]

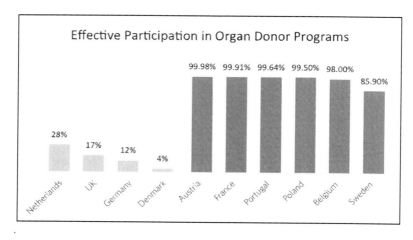

Figure 4.2: European country participation in organ donation

The four countries on the left have an opt-in for donor participation. That is, "Check the box if you want to participate in the organ donation program." Whereas the countries on the right have an opt-out, "Check the box if you don't want to participate in the organ donation program."

The Netherlands spent the most public money on campaigns to persuade people to participate, and got the highest participation rate among opt-in countries, but even that did not get them anywhere near the rates of opt-out countries. This is the power of status quo bias at work.

SUNK COST BIAS

When we come to making a decision, we often consider effort and work already done as a criteria for making a decision. For example, suppose ITC has already done a lot of work to determine how to make their customer service higher quality. This includes a plan to make the improvements and strong buy-in from staff to make this change. When ITC comes to decide which actions should be taken to meet the profit goals, should the work done on customer service be a factor in their decision? No. The question remains whether a higher quality customer service will create more profit. If you are emotionally invested in this option, can you see how easy it would be to argue for it? For example, "We can't stop now, otherwise what we've done will be lost." So beware: ask yourself, what decision would you make if you had not invested anything yet? Would you really watch the second half of the movie if you had not watched the first half?

ANCHORING

None of us start looking for information in a vacuum. We all have some preconceptions, including those based on views shared by others.

Decision science shows that we tend to rely too heavily on the first piece of information we hear. In practice this means that if, for example, we hear that competitors are focused on developing a certain technology, then we tend to look for information around that fact rather than looking more broadly.

In a price negotiation, the first person to name a price usually sets the range in which the final price will fall, as subsequent bids tend to oscillate around this first price. This means that being first to name a price for your next car, or for a company acquisition, is usually advantageous.

In their book *Blindspot: Hidden Biases of Good People*, Harvard Professor Mahzarin Banaji and University of Washington Professor Anthony Greenwald describe an experiment by Dan Ariely. He asked MIT students to write down the last two digits of their Social Security number and then to estimate the price of an item familiar to them, including a trackball.

Amazingly, the was a substantial correlation between the two sets of numbers when logically there should have been none. For example, those with the last two digits of their Social Security number between 0 and 19 said they would pay an average of $8.62 for the trackball. This price increased upwards until those with a Social Security number ending between 80 and 99 offered $26.18 for the very same item.

So my advice is that if you want to break for lunch at 1pm, then be the one to suggest it first and take suggestions from others as these are most likely to be in direct response to your suggestion of 1pm and who may suggest other times? rather than no lunch break at all.

CHECKING YOU HAVE MITIGATED FOR COGNITIVE BIASES

As you gather your information and fill in your dummy slides, step back and review the list of cognitive biases below. Do any need to be mitigated?

- WYSIATI
- Confirmation bias
- Availability bias
- Overconfidence bias
- Controllability bias
- Ststus quo bias
- Sunk cost bias
- Anchoring.

If so, what measure have you taken or will you take to mitigate the potential impact of the bias?

To rigorously innoculate yourself against these biases, a culture of constant awareness is required. To reinforce this, you can explicitly explain to the steering commitee the measures you undertake to keep yourself from falling into these flawed ways of thinking. This will raise both your own awareness and gives stakeholders permission to remind you of your intention should your awareness slip. Similarly, make it part of the modus operandi of the strategy design team to question how information was collated and what efforts were made to inoculate against biases.

SWOT ANALYSIS

With the important information about cognitive biases in mind, let's look at two useful analytical tools. The first is a SWOT analysis (Strengths, Weaknesses, Opportunities, Threats) which can be used as part of your diagnosis of the current situation. The idea is to assess information about your organization along the following four dimensions (your questions may already cover these):

- **Strengths** that the organization could pursue to its advantage

- **Weaknesses** of the organization that place it at a disadvantage relative to others

- **Opportunities** the organization could pursue to its advantage

- **Threats** to the organization that could lead to problems.

A SWOT analysis is often depicted in the form of a matrix and for each point you make in each of the four areas you need to have information to support your point of view. In particular, the opportunities and threats are likely to emerge from answers to the supporting questions on the current situation.

A SWOT analysis is often a helpful way to communicate insights about your organization and can be used to engage discussion and to align viewpoints.

Strengths	Weaknesses
• Long-standing and trusted relationships with over 1000 customers • Deep relationships with suppliers • Strong employee loyalty and retention • Effective sales model for serving large businesses	• Over reliance on large and medium business, with small footprint on small businesses • Limited innovation over past five years while competitors have introduced new offerings • Expensive sales models that are uneconomical for serving small businesses
Opportunities	Threats
• Introduce low cost, modularized offering for medium and small businesses • Expand business in Northern Europe, with focus on large businesses • Extend existing end-of-life recycling offer • Standardize process across BUs to reduce costs by 10%	• Continued pressure on pricing and margins with large businesses • Competitive threat if don't move fast to serve small businesses • Struggle to create a more cost effective model to serve small businesses, a default to more expensive model used to serve large businesses

Figure 4.3: Example SWOT Analysis for ITC

PESTLE ANALYSIS

The second analytical tool is PESTLE (Political, Economic, Social, Technological, Legal, Environmental). It can be very useful if your research includes looking in depth at the macro-economic environment in which your organization operates. PESTLE provides a way to organize your research and findings according to the following mnemonic:

- **Political:** analyzes the role of central and local governments in the economy. It typically includes comments on the stability of governments as well as commentary on tax, trade, labor and immigration policies

- **Economic:** analyzes expected economic trends including overall growth, inflation, interest rates and exchange rates

- **Social:** refers to social trends including those about demographics, consumer attitudes and lifestyle

- **Technological**: analyzes rate of technological change, expected technological innovations and available research funding

- **Legal:** analyzes legislation and regulation including employment, patent, and health and safety law. It also considers new legislation expected or planned that will affect the organization

- **Environmental[10]:** analyzes ecological and environmental aspects such as weather, climate and climate change.

Conducting a PESTLE analysis often makes sense if you want to compare opportunities in different geographies. This is especially so if the geographies you are considering are less known to your organization or if they are potentially fast-changing political and economic situations.

You can lay your PESTLE out as a matrix with six boxes, analogous to the format for the SWOT analysis. I also personally like a version that explicitly splits out commentary on each area and the expected impact and implications of it, as per the example for ITC in the UK which is overleaf:

Area	Expected trends	Expected implications for the organization
Political	• Stable UK government with pro business agenda • EU exit is possible with unknown implications for trade	• Nothing significant expected besides possible EU exit • If exit EU, consider locating more business in an EU country (vs in UK)
Economic	• Generally solid economy, subject to global trends (as per all countries) • Expect continued low inflation and interest rates • Dollar expected to maintain strength against the Pound	• Good economy means growing businesses which increases their IT needs, great for ITC • No other significant implications as not expecting big change from present
Social	• Population growth on average 0.7% 2004-2014, fastest in EU • Ageing population	• Since ITC's customers are businesses, consumer trends tend to have less impact

Area	Expected trends	Expected implications for the organization
Technological	• Fast innovation with digital economy, big data and Internet of Things • Technology done well is a key differentiator for businesses	• Ride on this trend to highlight need for technology • Also uses trends to improve services or reduce costs
Legal	• Legislation in part governed nationally, in part by EU, unless EU exit, in which case all will fall over time over UK law	• Nothing significant expected in short-term
Environmental	• UK likely to experience more extreme weather, e.g. flooding, in the future	• Need to ensure services mitigate risk of more extreme weather

Figure 4.4: Example PESTLE for ITC

FILLING IN YOUR DUMMY DECK

Once you have done your research and mitigated for biases along the way, you can fill in your dummy deck.

Good slide presentations rest on three things:

1. The **structure** of your presentation, as conveyed through order and titles of slides
2. The **content** of the body of each slide
3. The **design and formatting** of each slide

Structure:

To fully test for structure we require a bit more theory on structuring presentations which we will return to in Chapter 6. For now, it is sufficient to check for two things:

1a) Review the dummy slides in light of your findings, is there anything significant missing that requires additional slides, or anything that has become superfluous

1b) Have you followed the rule of one message per slide?

For each slide, ask yourself: what is the key message you want to convey? Is this conveyed by the title alone? Could the title be written more clearly, with each title kept to no more than two lines?

Content:

For the content of the body of each slide, you need to check that what is on each slide supports the title by providing evidence for it.

Be sure to select the most compelling pieces of information and present these on the body of each slide:

- Do not let yourself be limited by what you thought the supporting evidence would be when you drew up your dummy deck; if you have found more compelling information, use it

- Don't cram—if there is more relevant information on a subject than you expected, split it into two slides, each with its own key message

- Keep asking yourself if every piece of information on the slide is needed to support the title. If it isn't, discard it or place it in an appendix. Never include information just to demonstrate that you've done the work.

You also need to make each slide work standalone. By that I mean make sure that the key things the reader needs to know are clearly articulated on the slide. That way, anyone can pick up your slides and understand all the key messages without needing a voiceover.

Often when I teach this people don't like it. So I ask, have you ever given a presentation and then found that your slides were forwarded by email to someone who wasn't the meeting? Unless your answer is no, then remember that if your slides don't work standalone and you the recipient did not have the benefit of your voice-over risk gaps or misunderstandings.

I'm not recommending that you leave out details, anecdotes and stories in your voice-over, as these add further richness. I certainly don't want to listen to a presentation that is blandly read word for word, but if someone has to miss the meeting you want them to be able to understand the key messages of the presentation without being there and also without them needing a detailed explanation by you or by someone else who attended.

Design and formatting:

Don't underestimate the importance of the design and formatting of each slide. It can seem like a trivial point but it's not. The energy and attention the audience has to waste on trying to decipher poorly formatted slides is energy and attention that you would rather they use to focus on what really matters: the content.

Everyone is affected by how something looks. If a slide is well structured and easy on the eye, it's easier to take in. Understanding is significantly helped by consistent and simple fonts, colors and layouts. If you stick to this, then over time, no matter what the subject of the presentation, the audience will be conditioned to know what to expect and can better navigate the slides regardless of the subject matter. Such consistency also conveys a sense of professionalism that supports the effort put into the thinking. This includes making sure you have checked for typos, which may distract from content and can undermine your credibility, since sloppy formatting is often taken as an indication of sloppy thinking.

Effectively you want a situation where there is no distraction from the thinking. I remember a presentation early in my career, where I had an error in the numbers on one of the slides. I had a lackadaisical attitude toward formatting, as I believed that it was my ideas that mattered. However, the discussion got stuck on the wrong number, and never got back to the content and ideas I had been slaving over. The error was a typo rather than an error in calculation, but it put a question mark on the accuracy of all my numbers and by extension on my overall findings. With the credibility of my work in question, key ideas were obscured by the client's need to first understand and check the facts and figure out what it all meant by themselves. All the hard work I had put into it, only to be scuppered by a typo. Never again, I promised myself. Accuracy and formatting matters because it helps you get to what you want: the audience focusing on the thinking and your ideas.

KEY CONCEPT: GOOD SLIDE DESIGN

1. **Include one message per slide articulated as a "so what"**
   - Make the main message the slide title
   - Keep titles short, no longer than two lines
   - Don't try to highlight different messages in the body of the slide, use this space to support the main message.
   - If someone read the slide with no additional voiceover, would they understand the key points?

2. **Present data in a like-for-like way**
   - Use the same time period when presenting historical or future financial information. The mind gets confused if there is a revenue line chart for the past three years, followed by one for profitability for the past five years,

as it will first seek to compare the two lines assuming they cover the same period. In instances where this is not possible (for example lack of data) then explicitly point out the difference to your audience so they don't accidentally make an apples-with-apples comparison when it's an apples-with-oranges (or worse crocodiles) comparison.

3. **Be consistent in your use of frameworks**
   - If you use a framework to describe your findings, then continue to use this throughout. It is rarely helpful to use more than one framework in the same presentation and certainly you don't want to be using several.
   - For example, suppose in the early part of your presentation you articulate the criteria that you will use to make a decision. Let's say you use a slide with three boxes to the left and a description of each of these criteria to the right. Then later you describe five features of your customers, none of which have anything to do with the earlier three. This is confusing, use one or the other, or if needed build on the first to arrive at the second in a consistent way.

4. **Be consistent in your layout**
   - Once you have introduced a certain way of describing something or laying it out, stick with it.
   - For example, if you present a table of information with each year represented by a column, your audiences' minds will automatically assume this to be the case with future tables. So don't then include a table with each year represented by a row.
   - Similarly, if you are using a structure of boxes stacked vertically to the left-hand-side with text to the right, don't then shift to boxes placed horizontally with text beneath. Choose which format you want and then stick to it.

5. Be consistent in your use of color
- If you are using blue for revenue and green for profit, then do so consistently throughout
- The mind will automatically continue to associate the color with this information so don't make it more complicated by, for example, switching colors around on later charts or using a new color to represent the same thing.

6. Be consistent in your formatting
- Use a fixed layout for your slides
- For example use the same font and font size, margin widths, colors, boxes and layout throughout. This is also known as a slide master.

7. Keep slides sleek, clean and accurate
- Resist the temptation to try and convey too much information on one slide. Often less is more: choose the most impactful information and drop the rest (you can put it in an appendix if you want)
- Only include complicated graphics if they genuinely illuminate the message
- Double-check for typos and where possible ask someone else to proofread for you.

8. If a slide doesn't look right, redesign it until it does
- Remember that small changes can make a big difference in clean design
- Don't be afraid to scrap it and start again if it doesn't work.

DIAGNOSIS DOCUMENT

Following is an example of a filled in dummy deck for ITC is below. You might want to take a breather before looking through the slides, since at first sight the slides can seem a little dense.

Many of the slides will seem familiar as they are filled in versions of those from the dummy deck. Inevitably though as you do your research some titles and content in your dummy deck will materially change. For example, for ITC the dummy deck from a few pages ago has evolved to include:

• Additional slide: there was no slide referring to geographical source of revenue and profits; added as slide six

• Different order: moved the slide on organizational diagram slide to become the third slide for better flow, before then moving on to finance and customers

• Revised title for slide four: the title now refers to current revenue as well as revenue growth to ensure that the audience is anchored to the correct starting number, the time period of the chart was extended to five years to both match the date of the strategy and to give a longer historical precedent

• Revised title for slide seven: it turned out that profit numbers were actually flat over three years rather than having risen.

You could also add a SWOT analysis slide or PESTLE analysis slide here (although I have not in the ensuing example).

COMPLETED DUMMY DECK FOR ITC SOLUTIONS

ITC's mission is to be the leading reseller and IT services provider in North America and Europe

Mission Statement

To be North America and Europe's partner of choice for provision of IT products and services

Values

- Put the customer first
- Be expert partner to our customers, using technology to help their businesses to grow
- Have a collaborative and meritocratic work environment

Source: Company strategy documents

1

Its stated strategy, designed five years ago, focuses on being a reseller and not on services

Strategy 2011

- Grow share of large business segment products in North Americas
- Expand product business geographically across Europe from existing Western European base
- Develop and grow offerings for medium-size businesses in North America

Source: Company strategy documents

2

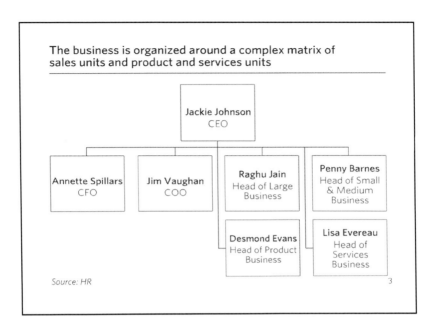

The business is organized around a complex matrix of sales units and product and services units

Jackie Johnson
CEO

Annette Spillars
CFO

Jim Vaughan
COO

Raghu Jain
Head of Large
Business

Penny Barnes
Head of Small
& Medium
Business

Desmond Evans
Head of Product
Business

Lisa Evereau
Head of
Services
Business

Source: HR

3

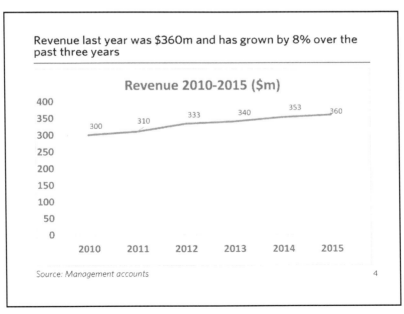

Revenue last year was $360m and has grown by 8% over the past three years

Revenue 2010-2015 ($m)

300 310 333 340 353 360

2010 2011 2012 2013 2014 2015

Source: Management accounts

4

This comprises 23% growth with medium size business and 4% decline with large business

Revenue split by Large, Medium and Small Businesses ($m)

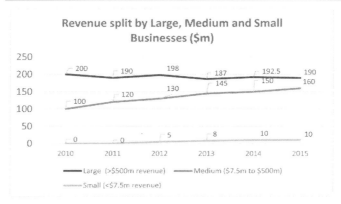

Source: Management accounts

5

80% revenue and 85% profit from USA

2015 REVENUE BY COUNTRY (%)

2015 PROFIT BY COUNTRY (%)

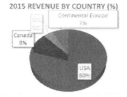

Source: Management accounts

6

Profitability has been flat past three years, with a fall in large business profits and a rise in small business

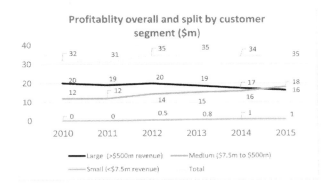

Projected profitability growth 1%, 10% and 10% by segment respectively per year, yielding $42m profit

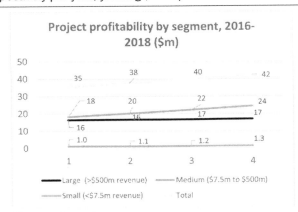

Today 17 customers (11%) generate 73% of our profitability

Customers and Profitablity 2016, ($m)

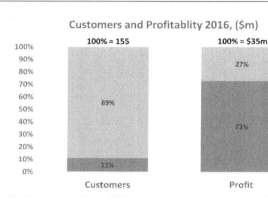

Source: BU Account lists; Management accounts

9

Of these 17 customers, 11 have contracts up for renewal in the next three years

Name	2015 Revenue	2015 Profit	Contract size	Start date	End date	Length	Due up next 3 years
Spectrum	45.6	4.1	250	Oct-11	Sep-16	5 years	Y
Handy Andys	41.4	2.9	180	Jun-15	May-17	2 years	Y
Bellview Hotels	19.1	2.1	120	Nov-16	Oct-16	3 years	Y
Johnsons and Co	14.6	1.9	200	Jan-15	Dec-20	6 years	N
Advantage	16.7	1.5	60	Feb-15	Jan-18	3 years	Y
Decorum	17.3	1.3	85	Dec-14	Nov-18	4 years	Y
Furniture World	16.4	1.2	100	Mar-15	Feb-19	4 years	N
Ashton Breweries	12.8	1.2	25	Jul-14	Jun-16	2 years	Y
Kirkton and Jameson	12.0	1.2	95	Apr-13	Mar-18	5 years	Y
Alexander Enterprises	12.2	1.1	65	Apr-14	Mar-19	5 years	N
Infinitum	12.9	1.1	60	Sep-12	Aug-16	4 years	Y
Generation X	10.5	1.1	70	Nov-14	Oct-19	5 years	N
Experience Holidays	12.2	1.1	50	Dec-14	Nov-18	4 years	N
Spotlight	12.5	1.1	50	Oct-13	Sep-17	4 years	Y
Excalibur	13.4	1.1	40	Feb-15	Jan-18	3 years	Y
Wainwright	12.3	1.0	50	Oct-15	Sep-19	4 years	N
Younjer Games	12.8	1	60	Jan-11	Dec-16	6 years	Y
Total	295	26	1560				
Contracts due next 3 years	217	19	1025				
%	73%	72%	66%				

Source: BU Account lists; Management accounts; interviews with sales staff

10

ITC's market share in small business—their biggest market— is less than 1%

MARKET SHARE, LARGE BUSINESS (%)

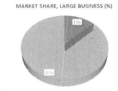

MARKET SHARE, SMALL BUSINESS (%)

MARKET SHARE, MEDIUM BUSINESS (%)

• No market share in US above 15%

Source: Management accounts; Gartner report on US IT market, 2016

11

Customer needs served today include technical expertise and speed of supplying products

Customer needs served today

• Provision of up-to-date information and technical expertise on latest technology
• Seamless supply of products and where required at significant speed
• Provision of IT services in a cost effective, reliable and seamless way

Source: Sales staff interviews; Customer survey 2015; Customer interviews

12

New needs include provision of modularized services and cost-savings share billing model

Unserved or new customer needs

- Provision of modularized services with the ability to buy these à la carte
- Creation of cost-saving share model where savings enabled through IT services are shared
- Rental of IT products
- Recycling of end-of-life products

Source: Sales staff interviews; Customer survey 2015; Customer interviews

13

No major regulatory changes expected although recycling regulations will increase needs

Expected regulation

- No expected legal changes affecting supply of products
- EU recycling regulation requires end-of-life equipment to be recycled and this creates a need which ITC could serve

Source: Department of Commerce; Internet searches

14

ITC has three major competitors, two of whom are growing fast

	ITC	Avantguard	Technology Partners	Minacon
Product and Services offering	• Primarily product • Large & medium businesses	• Primarily services • Mainly large businesses	• Products with some services • SMB focus	• Product & Services • Large & medium businesses
Key customers	• Spectrum • Handy Andys	• Bucaneer • Tyrus	• Agate Inc • Vox Industries	• Cyron Bank • Tagent Group
Revenue 2015	$360m	$550m	$320m	$425m
Profit 2015	$35m	$70m	$30m	$42m
Profit margin (%)	9.7%	12.7%	9.3%	9.9%
Revenue growth last three years	8%	25%	11%	2%
Profit growth last three years	0%	32%	7%	3%
# Employees	1250	2200	980	1400
Key locations	San Francisco, New York, Miami	Minneapolis, Boston, Los Angeles	Chicago, Austin, Los Angeles	Seattle, Boston, Austin

Source: Department of Commerce; company websites   15

Avantguard and Technology Partners' growth shows success with different customers

- Avantguard has continued to grow in revenue with large businesses largely due to focus on growing services market (versus stagnant product market)
- Technology Partners has made it easy for small businesses to trade with them by having a very easy to use and informative web shop and a 24-hour customer services line
- Both have picked a clear offering and target customers and then focused relentlessly on this

Source: Staff interviews; Company websites   16

DETERMINING SIGNIFICANCE AND IMPLICATIONS

Now that you have your base information in place, step back and ask: what are the implications of this information by topic area and taken overall?

For ITC, you would want to draw out implications on areas including:

- Whether existing **strategy and/or projected growth is sufficient to meet $50m profit goal** and if not, what the gap is likely to be

- Whether the **profitability % is stable or changing and why**

- Whether there seems to be **over- or underdependence on certain customer segments**

- Whether **needs are being met today and what are thegaps** and areas to explore to better meet these needs

- What **anticipated customer needs** and/or **changes in regulation** will need to be responded to

- Whether **competitor plans** create an increasing threat.

A good way to do this is to review your titles (i.e. findings) and draw out the implications. Be sure to only draw implications for which you have evidence—no point gathering all this information if you are going to diagnose without using it.

Following is an example Diagnosis Implications Table for ITC:

DIAGNOSIS IMPLICATIONS TABLE		
Area	Findings	Implications
Strategy	• ITC's mission is to be the leading reseller and IT services provider in North America and Europe • Its stated strategy, designed five years ago, focuses on being a reseller and not on services	• Strategy in need of revision to encompass plans in services
Financial performance	• Revenue past year was $360m and has grown by 8% over the past three years • Over past three years, this comprises 23% growth with medium size business and 4% decline with large business • 80% revenue and 85% profit from USA • Overall profitability flat past three years, created by falling profits from large business and increasing profits from small business	• Current projections fall short of three year profit target by $8m • Heavy reliance on USA for revenue and profit

Area	Findings	Implications
	• Projected profitability growth by segment is an average 1%, and 10% and 10% resp. per year, next three years, yielding $42m profit	
Customers and market share	• Today 17 (11%) customers generate 73% of the profitability • Of these 17 customers, 11 have contracts up for renewal in next three years • ITC's market share in the small business market, which is the biggest, is less than 1%	• Very heavy reliance on 17 customers with more than half of this revenue up for tender next three years
Customer needs	• Customer needs served today include technical expertise and speed of supplying products • New needs include provision of modularized services and cost-savings share billing model	• Opportunity to create modularized services offer, particularly for medium and small businesses and to explore offering a cost-savings share model
Regulation	• No major regulatory changes expected although recycling regulations will increase needs	• Opportunity to extend existing end-of-life recycling offer

Area	Findings	Implications
Competitors	• ITC has three major competitors, two of whom are growing fast • Avantguard and Technology Partners growth shows success with different customers	• Competitor success coming from focus on specific customer groups with targeted offerings (i.e. not trying to be all things to all men)
Overall		• To meet $50m profit goal, ITC will need to both successfully win contract renewals and extend range of services and extend share with medium businesses and/ or share with large businesses outside USA

Figure 4.5: Example implications table for ITC Solutions

MINTO PYRAMID PRINCPLE® TO STRUCTURE IMPLICATIONS

It is important to be able to show how you reach your implications. This is also about linking different pieces of information so your audience can understand the significance and implication of what you are sharing with them.

The Minto Pyramid Principle®, designed by Barbara Minto and described in her book *The Pyramid Principle*[11], is a way to clearly structure thinking and logic.

How would you remember the following shopping list?

Did you group according to category, as per Figure 4.6: dairy, fruit, vegetables? If so, this is very typical since the mind naturally categorizes into logical groups.

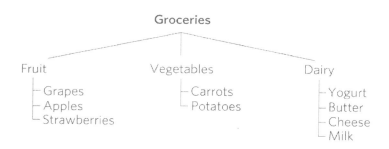

Figure 4.6: Minto Pyramid Principle® grouping according to category

We can draw this grouping in the form of a pyramid:

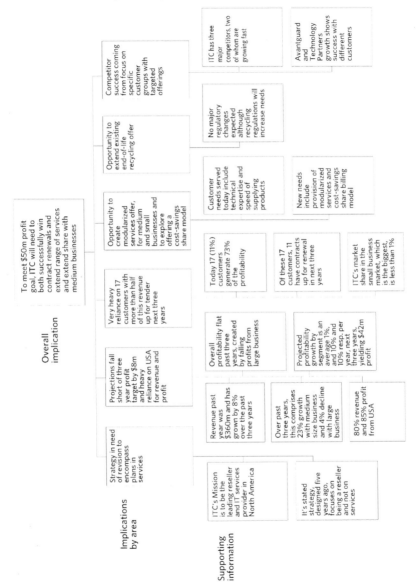

Figure 4.7: Implications in form of a pyramid

Applying The Minto Pyramid Principle® to the diagnosis, at the top you have the overall implications from the diagnosis, on the next row the implications by area and underneath supporting each of these the relevant information to be able to make that implication.[12] Similar to your question tree, replacing sub-question with idea then:

1. Ideas at any level need to build on the ideas grouped below

2. Ideas in each grouping need to be of the same theme or topic

3. Ideas in each grouping are in a logical order

4. No idea is a restatement of any idea beneath it.

DIAGNOSIS SUMMARY

You can summarize your findings by translating the pyramid into a prose summary. You can put this at the front of your *Diagnosis Document* and then add the slides containing charts as support behind. Take time to ensure every point is clear and precise, and reflect any changes you make in your slide titles as well.

Below is an example diagnosis summary for ITC:

To meet $50m profit goal, ITC will need to both successfully win contract renewals and extend their range of services, and extend share with medium businesses and/or share with large businesses outside the USA.

• Strategy in need of revision to encompass plans in services

• Current projections fall short of three year profit target by $8m

• Heavy reliance on USA for revenue and profit

• Very heavy reliance on 17 customers with more than half of this revenue up for tender next three years

• Opportunity to create modularized services offer, particularly for medium and small businesses and to explore offering a cost-savings share model

- Opportunity to extend existing end-of-life recycling offer

- Competitor success coming from focus on specific customer groups with targeted offerings.

If your audience remembers nothing else, make sure they remember this.

DIAGNOSIS CHECKLIST:

- You have produced a document that clearly lays out information needed for diagosis

- All sources of information are provided

- The information is based on facts and where this is not possible, a range of named interview sources

- You have mitigated for biases in the way in which you have sought, reviewed and presented the facts and evidence

- When you step back and read your summary, you are confident this provides a precise and objective diagnosis of the situation that is based on your findings (i.e. no reverting to what you expected the diagnosis to be unless that is fully borne out by all the facts).

5

GENERATING HYPOTHESES

*"Nothing is easier than self-deceit. For what every man wishes,
that he also believes to be true."*

Demosthenes

STRATEGY IN 5D

STEP	CHAPTERS
DEFINE	2. Defining your goal 3. Mapping the domain
DIAGNOSE	4. Diagnosing the situation
DEVELOP	5. Developing hypotheses 6. Testing hypotheses
DECIDE	7. Making choices 8. Writing your strategy 9. Communicating your strategy
DELIVER	10. Delivering your strategy

ACTIONABLE, RIGOROUS, COLLABORATIVE AT EVERY STEP (ARC)

KEY IDEAS

With your diagnosis in place, you are ready to address your next tranche of questions, which if you are using the Strategy in 5D question tree grouping, are the "options" questions. You can do this by working through each of the questions individually or through generating hypotheses for these questions.

Using a hypotheses-driven approach means that you test your best working assumptions of the answer, revising them according to the evidence you find until each can either be confirmed true or discarded. These working assumptions of possible options— possible answers to the set of sub-questions you have generated in that section of your tree—need to be written in a form that is meaningful, specific and testable. Working with such a set of hypotheses can save you a lot of time because it allows you to focus your information gathering activities in this phase on only the evidence needed tó prove or disprove the options you have identified.

A big note of caution: If you (or your key stakeholders) need an idea to be right once you have voiced it, do not use the hypothesis-driven approach. The hypotheses-driven approach only works if you are willing to be wrong and to discard your ideas in the light of new evidence. There is absolutely no place for dogmatism and sticking to a hypothesis regardless of whether the evidence supports it. If any of this is a concern, you are far better off answering each question comprehensively and getting to the right answer a little more slowly, than you would be using a hypothesis-driven approach. If you get too attached to your ideas, this approach will likely lead you to the wrong answers.

Do not underestimate the phase in which you test your hypotheses—it requires much rigor to ensure you test each hypothesis in an unbiased way.

This approach also requires some stamina—likely you will have to go through several iterations of the process for each of your hypotheses. It is perfectly normal to have to go through the cycle of gathering evidence, drawing insights, and revising your hypothesis for another round of testing three or four times before your hypothesis is spot on and you have enough evidence to either conclusively prove or disprove it (Figure 5.1).

Your hypotheses need to address all the questions relating to "options". This means you test all reasonable possibilities available to address the overall question, given the diagnosis. No need, at this stage, to develop hypotheses for other parts of the tree. You have already diagnosed the situation and you cannot develop meaningful hypotheses for the "choices" or "implementation" sub-questions as you need to have first determined what your options are to know what you are choosing from and then what you will be implementing.

Hypotheses are not facts. Until proven, they are open to questioning and probing by all. Only a rigorous, continued refinement of your hypotheses including at times totally discarding and replacing some of them, will lead to robust choices and ultimately a solid strategy. Don't let yourself be tempted into stating a hypothesis as a fact, no matter how confident you feel about it being right. If you don't yet have the evidence, it remains a hypothesis.

Your use of hypotheses may make colleagues nervous because they think that you have already decided what the answer is and that you are no longer open to alternatives. Look out for any signs of this and corral expectations. Clearly communicate your desire to understand the evidence, whatever it shows. Remind colleagues that you are not attached to the outcome or to a particular hypothesis being proven true—all that matters is what the evidence says. Demonstrate this mindset by being up front about it when the evidence does not support one of your hypotheses, no matter how much the hypothesis may have been lauded previously.

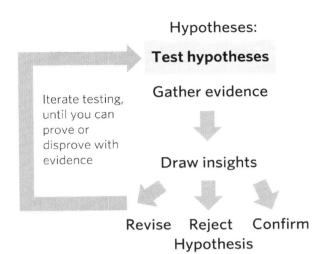

Figure 5.1: Hypothesis-driven approach: iterative phase

DELIVERABLES, CONCEPTS, ARC AND MEETINGS

Deliverables	• Hypotheses evidence table
Key concepts	• Specific, meaningful and testable hypotheses
Application of ARC	• Hypotheses are **actionable**, meaning they describe a concrete action which could be taken by the organization • Hypotheses are articulated with **rigor** and in a way that allows them to be tested. • Hypotheses are generated as a minimum **collaboratively** by the strategy design team and ideally with key stakeholders

Key meetings	Strategy design team: • Generate hypotheses via brainstorming session
	Steering committee: • If you have stakeholders with the time and drive to roll up their sleeves, conduct a joint brainstorming session with the strategy design team. Alternatively have a separate meeting with the key stakeholders as part of the testing and refinement process.

HYPOTHESES AS WORKING ASSUMPTIONS

Your hypotheses are your working assumptions of the best ways to address your "options" sub-questions, given your diagnosis. The approach here essentially is that even when you don't know the answers to your sub-questions, it helps to have some hypotheses as to what the answer could be to get started.

For ITC, example hypotheses of options could be:

• ITC needs to diversify its offering geographically beyond the US and has a good foothold for growth using existing services in Canada and Europe

• To be competitive to small businesses ITC would need a modularized product which can be bought à la carte

• To capture recycling opportunity, ITC needs to offer a full suite of recycling services

A good question to ask yourself as you put together your hypotheses is:

"What are my best working assumptions for the answer to these questions and how do I test if these assumptions are true?"

The hypotheses are tested and developed until you are satisfied that:

a) the evidence that is being used to prove or disprove the hypothesis is robust; and

b) the hypotheses will lead to a relevant, evidence-based conclusion.

If a hypothesis can't be tested as it's first written, rewrite it until you arrive at testable working assumptions, for example by breaking it down into components that can be tested.

SPECIFIC, MEANINGFUL AND TESTABLE HYPOTHESES

Hypotheses are statements, not questions, and they need to be written in a way that is specific, meaningful and testable. There is no point in generating fuzzy hypotheses, or hypotheses which, even if they are specific enough do not each provide a relevant and possible option for the organization. To confirm they are specific, meaningful and testable, ask the following questions:

Specific

• Is the hypothesis clear?
• Does it make sense on a stand-alone basis?

Meaningful

• Is it relevant?
• Does it make a difference whether it is true or not? (If not, then not relevant)
• If it were true, would it directly give rise to a tangible decision or action?

Testable

• Is it written in a way that allows for it to be proved or disproved by evidence? If not, can it be rewritten in a way that is testable, for example by being broken down into testable components?
• Can I find evidence with which to test my hypothesis?
• If I can't find irrefutable evidence, can I provide different pieces of evidence that when taken together suggest that the hypothesis is either true or not true?
• Is there a counterexample that would refute the hypothesis?

Here are a few examples of poorly written hypotheses that do not fulfill these criteria, and how each could be improved to make them specific, meaningful and testable:

Poor hypothesis	Why it's poor	Better hypothesis
ITC can improve marketing of international capabilities	Doesn't really tell us anything and certainly not the potential impact of this initiative. Verdict = not meaningful	By better marketing international capabilities to existing multinational customers in the US, can increase overall business by 50% in each of Canada, UK and Continental Europe
Small businesses are growing	Gives no idea of the relevance of this fact. In the previous example, the dots had been joined: small business growth matters because it is a big opportunity for ITC. Verdict = not meaningful	The creation of a modularized services offer, with flexible à la carte choice of services could increase US market share by 1% in each of small and medium business markets

Poor hypothesis	Why it's poor	Better hypothesis
Recycling regulation is increasing	This is a rather sweeping statement—are we saying this applies to all products and all customers? This could be a meaningful finding, but not as currently articulated. Verdict = not specific	Extend existing end-of-life recycling offer to add an additional 3% to revenue and profit

Review the following list of hypotheses and as you read write down your thoughts: Are they specific, meaningful and testable?

1. Our customers can be segmented.

_____

_____

_____

_____

2. We should focus on customers who are looking for a low cost offering to improve their profitability.

_____

_____

_____

_____

3. Our primary customer base needs a high-quality, efficient service and is prepared to pay a premium for it.

---

4. Revenue growth is important to restore ITC's profitability.

Please see the Appendix for comments on each of these.

APPROACH TO GENERATING HYPOTHESES

To develop an initial list of hypotheses, look at all the sub-questions relating to "options", then list what these options could be in a form that is specific, meaningful and testable. You don't need one hypothesis for each sub-question—indeed, you may have several hypotheses for one sub-question, or one hypothesis addressing several sub-questions.

Involve all key stakeholders in generating the hypotheses, both to get their ideas and their buy-in. You can do this either by inviting them to brainstorm with you, or by providing them with a preliminary list of hypotheses as a basis for discussion. Either way, hypotheses are dynamic, unlike the question tree, which once completed stays fixed. So be prepared for hypotheses to change and be refined both during and in between meetings as they are challenged and as you and your stakeholders learn more from the evidence gathered.

Like with the generation of sub-questions, it works well to run the generation of hypotheses as a brainstorm, with participants writing hypotheses on Post-it® notes and sharing with the group.

Participants should always write out each hypothesis in full so everyone can see it and comment on the wording to ensure it's precise.

Unlike your questions, that need to be MECE, your hypotheses don't need to cover every possible tenet and subset, in fact it would be incredibly difficult, if not impossible, to do this. Your hypotheses do, however, need to address all key and likely components of a solution. That is, your hypotheses, when taken together, need to provide a complete set of key working assumptions about the answer to the overall question.

Beware of creating too many hypotheses that are effectively testing a copy of what a competitor is doing. By all means there may be an opportunity to do something similar but better. For example, lower price, better service or enhanced features. Simply doing the same, however, creates no competitive advantage. Back to *Moneyball*: As Billy Bean, the manager of the Oakland A's says on whether to try and buy players like the Yankees do, but with less money, "If we try to play like the Yankees in here, we will lose to the Yankees out there."

At this stage, you want to generate more hypotheses than will ultimately make up your strategy, so don't limit yourself too early. Give yourself and your stakeholders enough material to make meaningful choices at a later stage.

HYPOTHESES AS A WAY TO PRIORITIZE

Hypotheses can provide a way to prioritize the work to be done. Often when you review your full set of hypotheses, two to three hypotheses will be pivotal to the direction of the answer to the overall question.

Taking the overall question as an example, you are looking for the best actions ITC can take to develop capabilities and achieve sustainable profit of at least $50m per year from 2018? That means a pivotal line of enquiry—unless this has already been closed off during the diagnosis—is to confirm whether this can come through cost reduction or must come primarily or even solely through revenue growth.

A starting point would be to assert a hypothesis on whether cost reductions can or cannot meet the profitability goal, for example:

- Cost reductions could save 25 percent of current cost base, sufficient to restore profitability, or,
- Cost reductions could at most total 10 percent of cost base and a minimum of 25 percent would be required to restore profitability.

With either hypothesis, the evidence you want is the same:
a) calculation of the level of cost reductions required to restore profitability within three years, and
b) reviewing costs by category and determining what cost reductions would be possible, likely within a range, for example a minimum and a maximum case.

This evidence would then either prove or disprove the hypotheses above. This also cues up the next hypothesis to be tested. In this example, either cost will have been shown to be insufficient to restore profitability and revenue growth hypotheses must be tested, or cost reductions are sufficient and further hypotheses need to be tested on what to cut and how best to do it.

CONFIRMING HYPOTHESES ARE TESTABLE

A good way to check that each hypothesis is testable is to identify evidence to test it with:

Testable hypothesis	Required evidence
By creating better international marketing capabilities to existing multinational customers in the US, it can increase overall business by 50% in each of Canada, UK and Continental Europe	• Talk to existing customers whom ITC serve only in USA to understand: a) Their satisfaction with current services b) Their needs outside USA c) How those needs are serviced today d) Whether they would be interested in ITC providing those services
Extend existing end-of-life recycling offer to add 3% to revenue and profit, i.e. $1m additional profit (based on average add to each customer)	• Services design team to spec out what extended services would be and their cost • Test with existing customers • Confirm financial potential based on feedback
By creating a robust webshop, can conduct 50% of product business online, saving $1m per year (after upfront investment costs to build – estimate $2m)	• Services design team to craft options for offer • Test with existing and potential customers

FUN EXERCISE: CHALLENGE YOUR HYPOTHESES

A fun exercise and one that can have great impact is to take the exact opposite of each of your hypotheses and try to find evidence to prove them. You can do this alone or, even better, with a group of people who have strong views on the subject.

Divide the group into smaller subgroups according to the differing hypotheses. Assign a hypothesis to each group, ideally where at least some of the participants do not agree with that particular hypothesis. Ask for evidence to support it and for this to be presented to the group.

This can have stunning results, as it cuts out "my idea" versus "your idea" fueled discussions, which can get mired in emotions. Instead, the focus is on proving hypotheses solely through evidence. This first-hand experience of arguing for another possible way forward is especially powerful for individuals with entrenched viewpoints.

THE ROLE OF INTUITION

I am often asked if the analytical techniques I teach preclude intuition. Absolutely not. The best problem solvers combine their intuition and gut feeling with a strong reliance on evidence and analysis. Generating solid hypotheses can draw heavily on your intuition and feeling for the answers to the problem. So don't hold back on using your intuition. The best operator I have worked with had an amazing commercial gut feel for what products and services would work, and what customers and suppliers needed. Yet, he was always open to evidence and facts to the contrary and in fact was grateful when these were brought to his attention so that he had a full view before making a decision.

DOCUMENTING YOUR HYPOTHESES

You can use a Hypotheses Evidence Table, like the following example, which contains the full list of hypotheses brainstormed for ITC. This example table covers the "options" questions four and five. Note that included is a running tally of the potential impact of the opportunities so as to be able to test whether the hypotheses could be sufficient to meet the overall goal.

Sub-questions	Hypothesis	Evidence	Owner & timing
Diagnosis: To meet $50m profit goal ITC needs to successfully win contract renewals and extend range of services, and extend share with medium businesses and/or share with large businesses outside USA to meet $8m gap from corporate plan.			
4. What opportunities are there to increase sales of existing products and services or to introduce new products or services?			
Current products & services to existing customers 4.1 What opportunities are there to provide more of the current products and services to existing customers and what could this deliver financially?	A. By better marketing international capabilities to existing multinational customers in US, can increase overall business by 50% in each of Canada, UK and Continental Europe • [worth estimated profit $2.6m per year (today outside US is 15% x 35m, so half again of this) less costs, which would need to calculate]	• Talk to existing customers who serve only in USA to understand a) Their satisfaction with current services b) Their needs outside USA c) How those needs are serviced today d) Whether they would be interest in ITC providing those services	Tyler Feb 1st

Sub-questions	Hypothesis	Evidence	Owner & timing
New products and services to existing customers 4.3 What new products or services could be provided to meet the needs of existing customers and what could this deliver financially?	B. For managed services customers, create a cost-savings share model • [need to add more detail to hypothesis and determine whether it has customer appeal and potential profit $Xm]	• Brainstorm with project team options for how this could work • Test options with customers for feedback	Saffron Feb 1st
	C. Extend existing end-of-life recycling offer to add 3% to revenue and profit, i.e. $1m additional profit (based on average add to each customer)	• Propositions team to spec out what extended services would be and their cost • Test with existing customers	Lydia Feb 1st
	D. Win three new contracts in next three years of at least $100m and min $3m profit per year ($1m each)	• Confirm financial potential based on feedback	Saffron Feb 1st

Sub-questions	Hypothesis	Evidence	Owner & timing
New products and services to new customers 4.4 What new products or services could we provide to meet the needs of new customers and what could this deliver financially?	E. The creation of a modularized services offer, with flexible a la carte choice of services could increase US market share by 1% in each of small and medium business markets (worth $3.25m additional profit)	• Proposition team to craft options for offer • Test with existing and potential customers	James Feb 1st
Revenue opportunities: Total first estimate impact to profit = $9.75m			
5. What opportunities are there to reduce costs and what would be the implications of this?			
Cost reduction opportunities 5.1 What cost reduction opportunities are there in how the customer is served?	F. By creating a robust webshop, can conduct 50% of product business online, saving $1m per year (after upfront investment costs to build— estimate $2m)	• Develop and test cost projections with finance team	Lydia Feb 8th

Sub-questions	Hypothesis	Evidence	Owner & timing
5.2 What cost opportunities are there through rethinking how we support customer-facing work?	G. Sell off slow moving stock more effectively to save $1m per year	• Develop and test cost projections with finance team	Tyler Feb 8th
Cost saving opportunities: Total first estimate impact to profit = $2m			
Overall suggests may be able to add the $8m to profit required from these hypotheses ($9.75m and $2m); all now needs testing.			

REVIEWING YOUR HYPOTHESES

Once you are comfortable that you have a robust set of hypotheses you can add the Hypotheses Evidence Table to the *Discovery Document*.

Step back and check three things:

• Is every hypothesis specific, meaningful and testable?

• Could these hypotheses provide a set of choices from which to form a strategy?

• Is anything missing from this set of choices?

Remember that unlike the Question Frame and question tree—that stay fixed—the hypotheses are designed to change. As you learn more you need to continually update your hypotheses, so that at any time any stakeholder could pick up the *Discovery Document* and review the latest list of hypotheses.

HYPOTHESIS CHECKLIST

- Each hypothesis is specific and makes sense on its own
- Each hypothesis is meaningful
- Each hypothesis is testable
- Taken together, the hypotheses cover the solution space. That is, the scope of a possible answer
- You continually evolve the hypotheses in the light of evidence
- You are willing at any time to discard a hypothesis which evidence does not support
- You brainstorm hypotheses as a project team and then continue to brainstorm and evolve them as you learn more
- You engage key stakeholders ideally in generating hypotheses, and if not, at least in reviewing suggested hypotheses.

6

TESTING HYPOTHESES

"I had, also, during many years followed a golden rule, namely, that whenever a published fact, a new observation or thought came across me, which was opposed to my general results, to make a memorandum of it without fail and at once; for I had found by experience that such facts and thoughts were far more apt to escape from the memory than favorable ones."

Charles Darwin

STRATEGY IN 5D

STEP	CHAPTERS
DEFINE	2. Defining your goal 3. Mapping the domain
DIAGNOSE	4. Diagnosing the situation
DEVELOP	5. Developing hypotheses 6. Testing hypotheses
DECIDE	7. Making choices 8. Writing your strategy 9. Communicating your strategy
DELIVER	10. Delivering your strategy

ACTIONABLE, RIGOROUS, COLLABORATIVE AT EVERY STEP (ARC)

KEY IDEAS

With a list of hypotheses in place, you are now in a position to test these. You are entering a phase of evidence gathering and review, and as already mentioned in the previous chapter, you will have to go through several iterations of gathering evidence, reviewing it, possibly revising your hypothesis and gathering and reviewing more evidence until you can either prove or disprove each hypothesis.

I affectionately call this the "washing machine phase" with the hypothesis being turned over and over, adding evidence as a sort of washing powder that cleans up your hypothesis. If, after multiple washing cycles with fresh washing powder (evidence), your hypothesis still does not come out clean (the evidence does not support it), then discard it and move forward only with the clean ones.

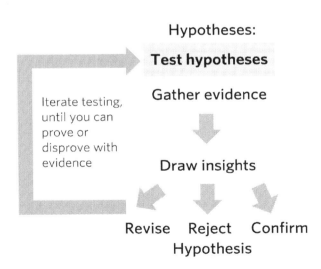

Figure 6.1: Hypothesis-driven approach: iterative phase

Your starting point confirming that you have identified the evidence you need to prove, or disprove each hypothesis. Be both precise and creative here: where are the best places to get the information you need? Who are the best people to talk to? Thinking laterally can help you gather a lot of valuable but harder-to-find information. Think of it as detective work.

You are likely to want to conduct:

1. **Desk-based research,** including insights from reports, interviews, quotes and numbers

2. **Interviews** with customers, competitors, market experts and staff, amongst others.

For each hypothesis, there are often two or three key pieces of evidence that prove or disprove it. At times you can identify these upfront. Other times, you may gather quite a bit more evidence than this and then realize the veracity of the hypothesis boils down to a subset of this evidence.

This is consistent with adopting an 80:20 approach, also known as Pareto's law. It states that 80 percent of the results come from 20 percent of the effort, so focus on the 20 percent of effort that will yield the most critical evidence.

For each and every piece of evidence you want to understand how reliable it is. Bear this in mind as you gather evidence—it may lead you to discard certain sources as less reliable or to decide to gather information from a larger variety of sources even during the initial gathering phase. You will inevitably end up discarding pieces of evidence because their source is not reliable enough or because you can find more robust evidence. Just be sure to document why you did not use a piece of evidence as this can be an invaluable record when someone asks you months down the track.

You then want to ask, "What is the evidence telling me?" Put aside your preconceptions and strive to see the evidence for what it is. An open, curious mind and really wanting to know the truth will serve you well here. The analysis of evidence needs to go beyond summarizing the information by drawing out the implications it brings with it. For instance, alone three pieces of data may say three separate things but when analyzed together they may provide insights well beyond those provided individually.

From the moment you start to gather and review your findings, document them as well. Take the time to structure your findings, update your hypotheses and identify any new information that is required. This will pay dividends in terms of the clarity of your own thinking and will provide a way to communicate progress to stakeholders. It also helps you sort through information and not get stuck on some detail at the expense of all the other pieces of information required.

Just as you did with the diagnosis, you want to identify how you will capture and display the evidence. The more you can define your end product upfront the more precise you can be in identifying the exact evidence you need—and don't need—thus making the most efficient use of your time.

The "develop" phase of Strategy in 5D and specifically this component of evidence gathering and interpretation, is the most time consuming of steps 1 to 4. You want to spell out upfront that this will take several weeks (in a ten week process typically no fewer than four) and provide a set of meetings at least once a week where findings are discussed. Given the likely duration and intensity of this phase, it is particularly important here to structure the work and agree on activities, responsibilities and due dates with the strategy design team to ensure everyone is on board.

Uncovering new information is rarely a linear process and it requires navigation. Multiple iterations help refine the richness and accuracy of the evidence, and as you inevitably discover some evidence you didn't expect, not only will your hypotheses need to be refined, you will also identify new information that then needs to be gathered.

DELIVERABLES, CONCEPTS, ARC AND MEETINGS

Deliverables	• Hypothesis findings tables • List of confirmed and rejected hypotheses • Prioritization matrix
Key concepts	• Summary versus synthesis • "So whats" • 80:20 rule (Pareto's Law)
Application of ARC	*Evidence* • Evidence is fairly and **rigorously** obtained from a wide range of sources • Evidence required is **actionable,** meaning sources for the evidence can be identified • Strategy design team **collaborate** to compile a list of evidence and this list is shared for input. Engage stakeholders in instances where can't identify evidence and want their input on possible sources *Findings* • Interpretation of evidence is **rigorous** and mitigated for cognitive biases • *Discovery Document* is **rigorously** updated to include findings, latest formulation of hypotheses and further information sought • Revisions to hypotheses are fair and **rigorous,** based on full review of evidence found • Revisions to the hypotheses ensure that they continue to be **actionable** • Findings are discussed **collaboratively**, with regularity and openness (no concealing of any information)

Key meetings	Strategy design team: • Initial meeting to review list of evidence and agree responsibilities. Twice-weekly meetings to share and review findings, reformulate hypotheses and ensure clarity on evidence still required
	Steering Committee: • Weekly or fortnightly meetings to share and review findings. Review implications of hypothesis revisions and list of confirmed and rejected hypotheses

IDENTIFYING EVIDENCE

For each hypothesis you need to list what evidence you will be seeking to test, and the source. Begin by reviewing the evidence list you compiled in the Hypotheses Evidence Table. Be upfront about gaps in evidence so you can return to these as your thinking develops.

Consider the usefulness of each piece of evidence or analysis as you go to avoid doing superfluous work. What insights could it provide? You may want to create a dummy deck to capture and structure findings, just as we did for the diagnosis. If so, follow the same approach as in Chapter 4, creating dummy titles for the slides and listing in the body of the slide the likely evidence to support the title.

DESK-BASED RESEARCH

For each hypothesis, consider what desk-research you could do to prove or disprove it, for example:

1. Are there reports written or numbers available that would provide quantitative evidence?

2. Are there published interviews with experts relevant to your hypotheses?

Get input from colleagues by asking them what evidence they would seek if they were in your shoes.

Desk-based research provides both standalone pieces of evidence and a base for further exploration in interviews. Here, don't limit yourself to using your research to inform interviews that you have already decided on—let it inform your choice of interviewees. Suppose you have found a helpful research paper, can you talk to the author and ask them to suggest further reading materials? Better yet, ask the author to point out an opposing opinion so that you can explore that with equal rigor.

As you gather your desk-based research, be meticulous in documenting all your sources and creating well-structured files of documents. At the time you might remember the source of each piece of evidence, but as you gather more evidence you will find it increasingly difficult to remember where each has come from.

INTERVIEWS

You also want to consider what evidence you will seek through interviews. They can provide richness and allow exploration and testing of a range of ideas and hypotheses that can complement your desk-based research. Quotes from interviews can be enormously powerful. Interviews may also provide the only evidence you can get in an area that is not data-rich.

The range of interviewees can include customers, employees, suppliers, competitors (often easier if conducted by an outside independent party) and industry experts. If you can find the right people and organizations to interview, you will start to see a web of information forming that will push you forward exponentially in your search for answers.

With so much information available on the internet, most data and information gathering does not need to be requested in advance. This is not the case for interviews, which tend to have a lead time of a week or two to book into people's calendars. As a result, it is best to set up interviews first and then use the time while you're waiting to continue your desk-based research.

Make sure you have a broad range of people to interview representing different views. New ideas, perspectives and lines of enquiry often arise when talking to others. Those who are not experts and who may therefore see things from a different perspective often open new windows of possibilities for you to investigate. You may need to reach out to more people than you intend to interview to secure sufficient interviews.

For anyone who feels a bit shy speaking to experts, don't be. Experts are most often delighted that you have read their work and would love to talk to you about it

At the time of requesting the interview, you don't need to know in precise detail what the interview will cover, just briefy explain the reason for the meeting and the major themes you want to discuss.

For example, if you were requesting an interview with one of ITC's customers to test the hypotheses, you could say:

"In response to your feedback, and that of other customers, we are looking to enhance our range of services, both in the US and possibly overseas.

Would you be wiling to meet for an hour so we can learn what else ITC could provide you with to meet your future business needs and to test some early ideas we have for extending our services?"

In some cases, it can also help to provide a list of the questions you intend to ask, so as to give interviewees the specifics to prepare.

KEY CONCEPT: GOOD INTERVIEW PRACTICE

Good interview practice is imperative to getting the most out of each interview.

Prior to the interview:

Write down your objectives: What is it you want from the interviews? What information do you need or what hypotheses are you testing? Ask yourself: "If this interview is successful what will I learn?" You don't want to leave the interview without having asked for what you need.

Draft an interview guide: This lays out the hypotheses you want to test and the questions you will use to do so. Include who will be doing the interview and give context for what you are doing. Don't ask leading questions and mitigate for cognitive biases. For example, you may tell someone a hypothesis and ask what evidence they have seen to support or refute it. Make sure you also have plenty of open questions and allocate time for new and unexpected information to arise.

Seek input on the interview guide: This not only enables stakeholders to add questions you may have missed and to challenge you on cognitive biases, but also gets their buy-in. You definitely don't want to conduct a set of interviews only for your stakeholders to later tell you that you missed some crucial questions, or worse, reject the findings due to their discomfort with the interview guide.

Send details of the interview to interviewee: Include the purpose, what to expect (possibly the questions), plus location and timing. You may also want to reconfirm the interview the day before.

If you don't know the interviewee, research the person you are meeting: Understand their background and any concerns the interviewee may have.

If you know the interviewee, put yourself in their shoes: Will they want detailed questions in advance? What might their perspective be? What might their concerns be?

Consider whether one or two interviewers is best: Two interviewers enables one interviewer to lead and the other to write notes, clarify the interviewee's answers and ask additional questions. One interviewer works best in a sensitive situation where the intimacy created by a one-on-one meeting can lead to a deeper and more frank conversation.

During the interview:

Give a proper introduction: Provide background about yourself, your objectives, and how the interview will work. Also discuss what feedback they may want from the interviews. For example, would they like to hear the overall findings once interviews are done? Give time for the interviewee to introduce him/herself (if not met before) and ask any questions about the interview.

Be clear how you will use the interviewee's comments: Establish with your interviewee beforehand whether they want their comments to be attributable or non-attributable. That is, whether you can refer to them in your overall findings or whether they would prefer to remain anonymous. You may also want to offer to share the overall results with them once the interviews are completed.

Use your interview guide as a guide, not a rigid structure: You want to make sure you cover all key questions, but you don't have to do this in the order of your guide. What's more important is to follow the flow of the conversation. Inevitably you will want to, and should, ask additional or follow-up that are that questions not on your guide. (Occasionally these are so good, you will want to add them officially to your guide for future interviews).

Remain aware of cognitive biases: Keep questions open and listen for cognitive biases in the responses to your questions as well as in your own formulation of the questions.

Re-cap at key points: Make sure you have understood the interviewee correctly. This also gives the interviewee the opportunity to add clarity and/or detail to their earlier response.

Ask if it's okay to follow-up post interview: You may think of additional questions or generate new hypotheses to test post interview. You also want to leave the door open in case something in the interview does not make sense afterwards.

Request introductions to other interviewees, as needed: The interviewee may be able to introduce you to other interviewees, especially once they have direct experience of what you are looking for.

After the interview:

Write interview notes: Be sure to take good notes and write them out while the interview is still fresh in your mind, within 48 hours. This may seem like a pain, but writing them helps crystallize and clarify what was said and identifies gaps for further exploration.

Follow-up: Write a thank you note. Leave the door open to come back to the interview should anything not make sense once you reflect on it or if you have further questions.

ADDRESSING EVIDENCE GAPS: MAKING ESTIMATES

The ability to make well-founded assumptions and estimates can cut through a hypothesis that is proving difficult to test.

Let's take an example. Suppose to test one of your hypotheses you need to know the annual demand for golf balls in the US. The key thing here is to be able to break this down into smaller components and make estimates from there. It works best if you identify:

- The inputs you are using to get to your answer
- The assumptions you are making about each input.

Inputs	Source	Assumptions
1. Population of US	US census	N/A
2. Proportion of population who play golf	Search online for estimates	X% (TBD) who play golf
3. Average number of balls purchased per player per year	Search online for information about average number of balls used Call a few golf stores or golf clubs and ask their opinion	Y balls per year per player
From here can take: 1.x2.x3. = estimate of number of golf balls sold in US annually		

Figure 6.2: Example estimates table

By making the assumptions transparent, people can see your thought process. It is helpful if you can check your estimates by finding more than one way of making the estimate (also known as triangulating). For example with finding out the number of golf facilities in the US, you could then research the average number of members per facility and then an estimate of the number of balls purchased per player per year. If they have questions or don't agree with the estimate, they can discuss this with you at the level of assumptions, rather than through the numbers alone, which can often be emotive, and lacking in the details of how you got there.

ADDRESSING EVIDENCE GAPS: WHAT YOU NEED TO BELIEVE

If you are struggling to identify evidence then an excellent approach is to ask yourself the question:

"What would I need to believe for X to be true?"

Let's take a couple of examples:

Example 1: Our business should invest in higher quality customer services.

As a business, for this to be true we would need to believe that:

- Investing in higher quality customer services would ultimately bring in more money. To test if this were true, we would need to understand:
  - What different levels of investment would mean for the quality of customer services. This could be mapped out with quality metrics/SLAs defined
  - What the impact would be on customers and how they might behave differently as a result. This could be tested with customers by simulating or describing a different level of customer service and gauging their response
  - If, in the past customer service quality was better or worse, how this affected income
  - If any colleagues have worked for a competitor, you could ask them how their customer service compared and weigh the impact of that versus your business' offering.
- You would also want to consider the opportunity cost of this investment versus others, including understanding:
  - What is the cost of upgrading customer services? Are there different options or one main option and hence associated costs?

- What else will it require, for example hiring of additional staff?
- Are there any factors that influence timing to do it now rather than at a later point?
- Overall, how easy or difficult is it to do?
- What else are we looking at doing and what would we not do if we did this?

It is worth remembering cognitive biases and in particular sunk cost bias here.

Suppose there is already a plan and lots of support from staff to make an investment in higher quality customer services, should this be a factor in the decision? No. The question remains whether a higher quality customer service will create more profit. Yet, if you are emotionally invested in this option, you can see just how easy it would be to argue for it with a, "We can't stop now, otherwise employee motivation and what we've already achieved will be lost, kind of attitude." Ask yourself, what decision would you make if you had not invested anything yet?

Example 2: We should expand our nonprofit's services from college scholarships to include job seeking and employment support.

To believe the above hypothesis to be true the things you should want to know include:

- That job seeking and employment support are services that are required by your users
  - Could ascertain this from the staff who most work with users, or through conversations or polls with users
- There is no other nonprofit or other organization already providing these services or who is better placed than your nonprofit to provide these services
  - Would need to profile skills and services provided by other organizations in similar domain

- That your nonprofit has the right foundations to build these skills
  - Map of current skills, skills required and any gaps that would need to be addressed
- That this is a more worthwhile opportunity than others the nonprofit could pursue
  - Then list all other possible opportunities and quickly evaluate along two dimensions: 1. Likely impact and 2. Ease of implementation. A good way to compare them is by plotting them on a Prioritization Matrix (see Figure 6.3)

Prioritization Matrix

	Low ——— Ease of Implementation ——— High
High Impact	Opportunities you may want to pursue — they will yield a lot but will be difficult. / Opportunities you want to pursue — high impact and easy.
Low Impact	Opportunities you do not want to pursue — low impact and difficult. / Opportunities you may want to pursue — less impact, but easy to do and quick results, builds morale.

Figure 6.3: Matrix to prioritize opportunities by impact and ease

166

REMAIN AWARE OF CONFIRMATION BIAS

Look out for your own confirmation bias at all times during the hypothesis testing process, and acknowledge that your judgment can be easily clouded by it.

Play the a devil's advocate and explore what you would need to believe for the opposite of your hypothesis to be true. Seek evidence that would prove its opposite.

Avoid the impulse to adopt a default position on anything.

Talk to people who don't share your views. Seek to understand their views. Suppose you take the opposite viewpoint to your hypothesis, what would you have to believe for it to be true?

DOCUMENTING YOUR EVIDENCE

Document your findings and the resulting revisions to each hypothesis in your *Discovery Document*. I recommend that you add a page for each hypothesis and structure it as per the following, providing space for documenting your findings and thinking. I call these my Hypothesis Findings Tables.

HYPOTHESIS FINDINGS TABLE: EARLY FORMATION	
Original hypothesis	Better international marketing capabilities to existing multinational customers in US, can increase overall business by 50% in Canada, UK and Continental Europe Worth estimated profit $2.6m per year (today outside US is 15% x 35m, so half again of this) less costs, which would need to calculate
Revised hypothesis	TBC
Implications ("so whats" of evidence)	TBC

Evidence	• Of three interviews with existing customers with operations in at least one of Canada, Germany and the UK, two said they would be seriously interested in doing business there, with the same products/services and terms in the US
	  – [Interviews with Bellview, Infinitum and Generation X]
	
	• No regulatory restrictions since already have some operations in each of the three countries
	  – [Confirmed by legal team]

Further evidence sought	• Interviews with at least five more multinational customers to test interest • Forecast market growth rates by country • Modelling of potential profitability based on interviews

Unused evidence / Other hypothesis formulations	• Regulatory rules for Canada, Germany and UK

Make sure you update your hypotheses in response to the evidence. If you find surprising evidence, be prepared to shift course. If the evidence disproves the hypothesis be prepared to stop pursuing that avenue of thought altogether. Sticking dogmatically to a hypothesis despite evidence to the contrary is an absolute no-no.

Make assumptions explicit. When you use evidence, particularly numbers, you will need to make assumptions. For example you might need to calculate the size of a market and need to split an existing known market size into several components. Resist the temptation to position the market sizes coming from this as fact. Explain the assumptions behind how you have split the market into the different components as well as the resulting market size number this yields. If you are making forecasts and projections or you use forecasts developed by others, make sure you spell out the assumptions behind these.

You need an investigator's mindset and you must be ready to back-up every assertion or assumption at any point. It's a horrible feeling when you are asked for your earlier hypotheses, or for evidence or sources of your evidence six months later and you just can't remember.

So keep a record of older formulations of your hypotheses, as well as of all evidence and all sources. This will also help you to not only arrive at a set of confirmed hypotheses but to always be able to retrace and share the path that got you there.

It's also a good idea to keep a note of sources you later discarded, so that if at a later stage you are asked whether you reviewed a certain source, you will have a record of this.

In the Hypothesis Findings Tables, to distinguish between evidence and sources, I put the sources in square brackets; you don't need to use this formatting but I do recommend you find a way to clearly distinguish them.

INTERPRETING YOUR EVIDENCE

The interpretation of your evidence is a crucial step that shapes your whole strategy. You need to be very thorough in your treatment of each piece of evidence. This is not a simple box-checking exercise where you get the evidence and you are done regardless of what it says. Question it. Perhaps the data does not tell you what you expected it to, but see it for what it is.

Always perform a sanity check on your data. If the evidence looks wrong, then it probably is. If you have any doubts at all, review the evidence and any assumptions again. For example, if according to your calculations the annual demand for golf balls in the US comes out at 60bn (i.e. 200 balls per person), ask yourself if this seems sensible or if there is a mistake somewhere.

Put WYSIATI into practice by not half glancing at your evidence and assuming it says what you were expecting. What does it really say? Does it really prove or disprove your hypothesis? Perhaps, it suggests that the hypothesis needs to be revised and then tested further. Or does it provide a final piece of evidence that confirms an hypothesis?

Don't be afraid to discard evidence. You don't need to show all the evidence you have gathered. Resist wanting to show how much work you have done and instead focus on communicating your most striking findings. You will want to discard—or place in an appendix—evidence that is not robust or evidence that becomes superfluous due to better evidence.

Above all, be honest about what the evidence is telling you, and don't allow yourself to make assumptions on scanty or conflicting evidence or allow cognitive biases to mask the true meaning of the evidence.

EXAMPLE: INTERPRETING EVIDENCE

Let's return to example 1 earlier in this chapter, the hypothesis that it is worth investing in higher quality customer service.

Suppose that the customer interviews reveal that customers are happy with the service they are receiving. Indeed, on average they rank the service they receive as better than that of competitors. Suppose also that during the interviews several customers raise an issue they are experiencing with one of our products and initial feedback suggests that this is losing us money.

Report back to your stakeholders what you have heard and and that there is no evidence to support the hypothesis.

Then ask that your effort can be pivoted to investigate the product issue that customers are highlighting to determine what actions should be taken.

"SO WHAT?" DETERMINING THE IMPLICATIONS

Two words used constantly at McKinsey are "so what?" Or in other words, "What are the implications of what you have found?"

McKinsey consultants typically ask themselves and their team "so what?" dozens of times a day as they sort through the myriad of data and evidence.

A "so what" is more than a summary of the evidence. It is a synthesis of the evidence which draws out the implications of the evidence. The following table provides examples of the difference between summary and synthesis:

Summary = Grouping of facts and ideas	Synthesis = Pushing for "so what" and implications from key ideas and evidence
Needs of customers vary; some are common, some not	Customer's needs are not homogenous with four clear segments emerging
Using computing language R provides more control	By not using computing language R, we miss out on time savings, faster response and a greater range of experiments
New landing pages are making a difference	New landing pages are adding $100M of revenue to the business and could drive a further 10% uplift, worth approximately $200m revenue

Figure 6.4: Summary versus synthesis

One approach is to quickly write down all the key insights from your evidence and then test and rewrite them into punchy "so what?" lists. Use the following questions to refine your "so whats":

1. What is the evidence really telling me, both standalone and when I combine with other pieces of evidence. Is this the most I can reasonably infer?

2. Is the "so what" saying something meaningful or is it more likely to only elicit a disinterested "uh-huh?"

Then once you have a refined list of "so whats", ask two further questions:

3. What impact does each "so what" have on the hypotheses? Which need to be revised or discarded as a result? Is there anything significant enough to be flagged to stakeholders prior to our next meeting?

4. What impact do the "so whats" have on further evidence required and/or the direction of evidence gathering?

As you review all your "so whats", be sure that all are reflected in revisions made to hypotheses and ultimately in the final list of confirmed hypotheses.

PLAY THE "SO WHAT" GAME

If you are stuck and feel like your "so what" isn't saying enough then read out your "so what" to a colleague and get them to repeatedly ask you "so what", each time refining the "so what" like peeling an onion. Here's how it might go:

You: Basically, I'm just saying that customer service is important to our customers.

Friend: So what?

You: Well, it is important because it has a bearing on how easy it is to work with us and how much they want to do. Often customers contact our customer services department when they are new to us and these first experiences can determine if we become good business partners or if the relationship dwindles before it has even started.

Friend: So what?

You: Oh well, it's important as I said. But in fact our customer service is pretty good and on average as good as our competitors'.

Friend: So what?

You: It means that we should always monitor that our customer service is good enough and that there is nothing we need to do right now, no further investment required, our current service is good enough.

DOCUMENTING YOUR "SO WHATS"

Use your Hypothesis Findings Tables in your *Discovery Document* to record your "so whats" in the implications section and the supporting evidence and revised hypotheses in their sections too.

HYPOTHESIS FINDINGS TABLE: MIDWAY FORMULATION	
Original hypothesis	By better marketing international capabilities to existing multinational customers in US, can increase overall business by 50% in each of Canada, UK and Continental Europe [Worth estimated profit $2.6m per year (today outside US is 15% x 35m, so half again of this) less costs, which would need to calculate]
Revised hypothesis	By targeting existing customers with operations in Canada, Germany and the UK and by setting up local sales teams in each of these countries, can at least double profitability in all three markets by end 2018 This is estimated to yield an additional $1m profit per each of the three countries by 2018. Total additional per annum by 2018 = $3m
Implications ("so whats") of the evidence	• Established need for our services overseas with customers who trust us plus growth overall in these markets, suggesting opportunity also for new customers • No legal impediment to building business in any of Canada, Germany and UK

Evidence & sources	• Of six interviews with existing customers, each of which who have operations in at least one of Canada, Germany and the UK, five said they would be seriously interested in doing business with ITC there, with same products/services and terms as in the US
	   – [Interviews with Bellview, Infinitum and Generation X]
	• All three are growing markets in services of at least 3% per year
	   – [Analyst reports: Gartner, UBS, Morgan Stanley]
	• No regulatory restrictions since already have some operations in each of the three countries
	   – [Confirmed by legal team]

Further evidence sought	• Interviews with at least two more multinational customers to test interest • Modelling of potential profitability based on interviews
Unused evidence / Other hypothesis formulations	• Regulatory rules for Canada, Germany and UK

I think of the *Discovery Document* as my loyal friend—it stores my best thoughts and findings, remembers all the things I would otherwise forget, reminds me what further research I need to do and by reminding me constantly of the question I am seeking to answer, it makes sure I can't go too far off track. Updating the *Discovery Document* helps clarify my thinking and make sense of all the new information I am absorbing.

It also provides an excellent communication tool for the strategy design team and for updating your steering committee. During the middle weeks of the strategy design process—typically weeks six through ten of a fourteen week process—the *Discovery Document* provides the backbone for all discussions with the strategy design team and with the steering committee. It gets the important points across without requiring the strategy design leader or team to spend half the week prior to the steering committee meeting on writing a PowerPoint deck, time that would be much better spent on gathering and reviewing new information.

At times you will have really striking insights that would come out better in the form of a chart. In this case, there is of course nothing to stop you from creating a chart and inserting it into the *Discovery Document.*

The time you invest in a well-structured and maintained *Discovery Document* will pay off when you come to make choices and craft the story of these choices and of the resulting strategy.

CONFIRMING YOUR HYPOTHESES

As your evidence builds, you want to determine when you have sufficiently proved or disproved a hypothesis.

You need to be confident that your findings are robust and supported with evidence. In some cases, you can get evidence that immediately proves or disproves a hypothesis. For example, suppose you have a hypothesis that suggests entering a certain geographic market, then suppose that you find that this market is well-served, customers are happy, the businesses serving them are not making much money and you would need special licenses to work there that typically take two years to obtain. All this points very strongly to disproving the hypotheses.

But often the reading of the evidence is more nuanced. For example, what if customers were not well served and the businesses operating there were making a lot of money. Notwithstanding the license issue, would it still be worth entering the market?

In such a case, it is often through first iterating and getting additional evidence and then reviewing all the evidence and its implications to weigh the evidence overall. This can then be used to determine if a hypothesis is true, not true or partially true and needs to be revised.

You want to make sure that all your key "so whats", that is the insights from your evidence, are reflected in your final articulation of the hypotheses. Where they are of a lesser importance, include them in the supporting evidence.

You also need to know when to stop gathering evidence, when what you have is good enough.

Be aware of curiosity for the sake of curiosity. Doing research and gathering new evidence is not necessarily the most effective use of time and can mean your intellect is taking over, with evidence at the expense of practical outcomes. While I am a huge fan of facts, there is undoubtedly a balance to be struck between:

- Judiciously chosen pieces of evidence, versus
- A sea of evidence that has quantity but not necessarily quality.

Two key tactics to avoid this are:

1. Keep seeking to identify the two or three pieces of information on which the hypothesis turns and;
2. Remember the 80:20 rule and keep applying it to the work to be done and evidence to be gathered.

If you want to research something simply because you want to, there is nothing wrong with that. Just be clear to call it what it is and be sure not to prioritize this work above that which is absolutely required.

Once you are confident in your final formulation of the hypothesis, it becomes a confirmed hypothesis. Taken together, the confirmed hypotheses provide the set of opportunities from which you will make your choices.

So step back one last time and check the hypotheses that you are confident you can confirm and the hypotheses with evidence to disprove them. Finally, check you have not overlooked any hypotheses where the evidence is not yet there and where further work is required. If there are hypotheses requiring further testing, then keep going until you can confirm or disprove. Then provide a final precise articulation of all your confirmed hypotheses: the opportunities from which you'll create your strategy.

THE PARETO PRINCIPLE — THE 80-20 RULE

The Pareto Principle, also known as the 80-20 rule, describes how roughly 80 percent of effects come from 20 percent of causes.

It was named after Italian economist Vilfredo Pareto, who observed in 1906 that 80 percent of the land in Italy was owned by 20 percent of the population. He further developed the principle by observing that 20 percent of the pea pods in his garden contained 80 percent of the peas.

In business this can mean:

- 80 percent of your revenue comes from 20 percent of your clients
- 20 percent of your staff will provide 80 percent of your production
- 20 percent of your staff will cause 80 percent of your problems.

Applying this to evidence, it means that 20 percent of your evidence will provide 80 percent of your insights. As you write your workplan, consider: What are the key pieces of evidence that will yield the most important insight(s)?

Thinking 80-20 helps you avoid seeking superfluous evidence, and saves you from unnecessary use of your and your employees' time and efforts.

HYPOTHESIS FINDINGS TABLE: FINAL FORMULATION	
Original hypothesis	Better international marketing capabilities to existing multinational customers in US, can increase overall business by 50% in each of Canada, UK and Continental Europe
	[Worth estimated profit $2.6m per year (today outside US is 15% x 35m, so half again of this) less costs, which would need to calculate]
Confirmed hypothesis	By targeting existing customers with operations in Canada, Germany and the UK and by setting up local sales teams in each of these countries, can at least double profitability in all three markets by end 2018
	This is estimated to yield an additional $0.8m profit per each of the three countries by 2018.
	Total additional per annum by 2018 = $2.4m
Implications ("so whats") of the evidence	• Established need for our services overseas with customers who trust us plus growth overall in these markets, suggesting opportunity also for new customers
	• No legal impediment to building business in any of Canada, Germany and UK

Evidence	• Of eight interviews with existing customers with operations in at least one of Canada, Germany and the UK, five said they would be seriously interested in doing business with the same products/services and terms as in the US
	  – [Confirmed interviews with Bellview, Infinitum, Generation X, Spotlinght, Excaliber, Wainwright, Furniture World, Decorum and Spectrum
	
	• All three are growing markets in services of at least 3% per year
	  – [Supported by analyst reports: Gartner, UBS, Morgan Stanley]
	
	• If ITC could win just 20% of their business this would equate to a doubling of our profitability in those countries
	  – [Confirmed by finance team]

Evidence	• No regulatory restrictions since already have some operations in each of the three countries – [Confirmed by legal team]
Further evidence sought	• N/A
Unused Evidence / Other hypothesis formulations	• Regulatory rules for Canada, Germany and UK

FINALIZING LIST OF CONFIRMED HYPOTHESES

Once you have completed the work and final Hypothesis Findings Table for each hypothesis—meaning you have determined whether each can be confirmed or rejected—then add a complete list of these to your *Discovery Document*. Where needed, include the expected impact as this will be needed to assess whether there are enough options with which to reach your goal. Below is a list of confirmed hypotheses for ITC and following, a list of rejected hypotheses:

CONFIRMED	
Confirmed hypothesis	Estimated impact
A. Overseas sales teams: By targeting existing customers with operations in Canada, Germany and the UK and by setting up local sales teams in each of these countries, can at least increase double profitability in all three markets by end 2018	This is estimated to yield an additional $0.8m profit per each of the three countries by 2018. Total additional per annum by 2018 = **$2.4m**

Confirmed hypothesis	Estimated impact
C. Recycling: Offer cradle-to-grave recycling modularized services for all hardware including that not purchased from ITC, service includes filing of all associated paperwork	Assume can win $20k per year of recycling services with 50 customers by 2018 = $1m revenue per year Revenue from metal traders, assuming 2018 original value $0.5m per customer, @ 50 customers = $25m equipment, @30% = $7.5m of equipment, sold @10% = $0.75m Cost to deliver services = 6 people x $100k average fully-loaded salary = $600k Estimated profit per year in 2018= $1m +$0.75m -$0.6m = **$1.15m**
D. New contracts: Win three new contracts of at least $75m and $2m profit per year	In strong position to win at least three new contracts of at least $75m Assume $0.93m per contract per year, reduced by 30% to $0.66m per contract per year Profit per year = **$2m**

Confirmed hypothesis	Estimated impact
E. Modularized services: The creation of a modularized services offer, decoupling existing services packages, and with flexible à la carte choice of services	**With a webshop in place,** this would increase ITC's medium business by at least 20% and double small business. This would generate $4.15m profit per year less additional advertising costs of $250k, yielding **$3.9m per year additional profits** **Without a webshop,** and assuming an increase of small business by 30% and medium business by 10% this would generate **$2.1m per year additional profits**
F. Webshop: By creating easy to navigate webshop, can increase small and medium business by 5% and conduct 80% of small and medium business and 40% of large business online	This will increase profits by $1m due to extra revenue and a further $300k due to cost savings in field sales force = **$1.3m additional profit per year**
Total Estimated Impact	Up to a maximum of $10.8m

REJECTED	
Rejected hypothesis	Estimated impact
B. Cost-savings share: For managed services customers, create a cost-savings share model	N/A
G. Slow moving stock: Sell off slow moving stock more effectively to save $1m per year	N/A

You can reorder the confirmed hypotheses based on estimated impact. In the table below for ITC, since there are different estimates for modularized services depending on whether the webshop is built or not, these are listed both together as E. & F. and individually as E. and individually as F.

You can also map out the ease of implementing each hypothesis:

Confirmed hypothesis	Estimated impact	Ease of implementation
E & F. Modularized services and webshop	$5.2m	Low/Medium Requires marketing effort to modularize existing packaged services; limited redesign required. Also requires technical build of webshop
A. Overseas sales teams	$2.4m	Medium Requires recruiting new sales staff in each of Canada, Germany and the UK, where already have operations

Confirmed hypothesis	Estimated impact	Ease of implementation
E. Modularized services without webshop	$2.1m	Medium Requires marketing effort to modularize existing packaged services; limited redesign required
D. New contracts	$2.0m	High Good track record in winning business and team already in place with capabilities to deliver this
F. Webshop without modularized services	$1.3m	Low/Medium Requires significant technology build which can be built alongside existing webpage for minimal disruption, but need to carefully manage design and functionality to ensure result is what customers need
C. Recycling	$1.2m	Low/Medium Already have thorough understanding of regulation; some design work to determine full set of services required to be cradle-to-grave

You can then plot them on the prioritization matrix, as per the following, displaying all feasible options from which choices for your strategy will be made.

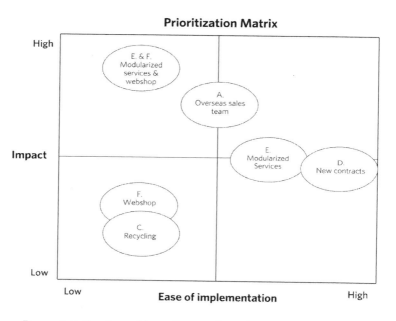

Figure 6.5: Confirmed hypotheses plotted on prioritization matrix

TESTING HYPOTHESES CHECKLIST

- Relevant evidence has been identified to test each hypothesis or to answer each supporting question
- You are aware of confirmation bias and take measures to mitigate it
- Sources are provided for each piece of evidence
- The range of sources is broad and often encompasses both data and interviews
- Where assumptions have been made, these are explicit
- Fair implications are drawn from the evidence.

7

MAKING CHOICES

"Life is the sum of all your choices."

Albert Camus

STRATEGY IN 5D

STEP	CHAPTERS
DEFINE	2. Defining your goal 3. Mapping the domain
DIAGNOSE	4. Diagnosing the situation
DEVELOP	5. Developing hypotheses 6. Testing hypotheses
DECIDE	7. Making choices 8. Writing your strategy 9. Communicating your strategy
DELIVER	10. Delivering your strategy

ACTIONABLE, RIGOROUS, COLLABORATIVE AT EVERY STEP (ARC)

KEY IDEAS

Strategy is about choices: what you choose to do—and what you choose not to do—to take you from where you are today, to where you want to get to. You have rigorously tested each hypothesis and have determined which of these can be confirmed as options to meet your overall goal. With this set of options you are now ready to put together your strategy: it's time to decide.

Your first step is to determine if collectively, you have sufficient options to meet the goal expressed in your overall question. There are three possibilities:

1. Considered collectively, the estimated impact of your options is **insufficient** to meet your goal. In this instance, review whether there are any additional hypotheses you can test as potential options. Do not, however, try to find reasons to re-introduce a hypothesis that you had already legitimately ruled out. You want a strategy that will work based on genuine, verified hypotheses. If there just aren't any additional feasible options, then it's better to revise the original goal.

2. Considered collectively, the estimated impact of your options is **just sufficient** to meet your goal. Provided it is practical, you are likely to want to pursue all these options, albeit sequenced to ensure sufficient focus on each for success.

3. Considered collectively, the estimated impact of your options is **more than sufficient** to meet your goal. Your next step is to determine which of these you will pursue.

Part of this consideration is an evaluation of each hypothesis to determine how much each has the potential to deliver and how difficult each will be to implement as per the Prioritization Matrix derived in the previous chapter.

The Prioritization Matrix works well at the level of assessing an individual option. It is not however sufficient when choosing a set of options. Thought must also be given to potential synergies or conflicts between options as most importantly you want a set of options that work well together as a program of work:

- Which set(s) of options provide more than just the sum of each individually?

- Which options draw on the same resources in a helpful way?

- Which options draw on the same scarce resource?

- Which options do not definitely go well together?

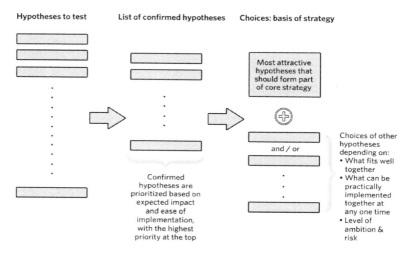

Figure 7.1: From hypotheses to choices

The best choices come from reviewing the different combinations of options, what these could deliver and collectively, how difficult these will be to deliver. This means that you will not necessarily be choosing the top three options as prioritized individually. Suppose now that option one is in conflict with both options two and three. Then your feasible set of choices are likely combining options one with options four onwards, or combining options two and three, with options from four onwards, and it is one of these sets of options which should form your strategy.

Remember, strategy is about choices and as much about what you choose not to do as what you choose to do. Be realistic about how much your organization can do at any one time. You need to weigh-up your options and the sequencing of these chosen options. Choosing not to do something now does not mean you will never do it. You can return to these on-hold options in a year or two when you have successfully delivered other options.

Be sure to schedule sufficient discussion time with the strategy design team and with wider stakeholders to debate the choices. Given you have done all this hard work to generate and test hypotheses, make sure that your choices are based on the results of this. Do not inadvertently revert to opinions you or others held before you began the strategy design process.

You also want to schedule sufficient time to craft your communication of these choices. All of us have had to sit through presentations that are poorly structured or contain badly written slides. If a presentation is hard going or there are things that are difficult for the audience to follow, you will quickly lose them. A lost audience means there is no chance of them leaving feeling inspired or excited to talk about it with colleagues, let alone wanting to mention it to the CEO the next time he or she asks what important and exciting things are going on.

You want to communicate the strategy in the form of a story, whereby you logically explain how you got to the choices and the findings that support these choices. An excellent way to structure your story is to use the Situation-Complication-Resolution Framework (SCR) which uses The Minto Pyramid Principle® as its backbone to provide a pathway from starting point to desired end point. Situation describes the context, Complication describes your diagnosis and the Resolution explains the choices you propose and the rationale for choosing these options over others. The SCR Framework is outlined in full later in this chapter.

The great news here is that you have already done most of this work; what remains is to finalize any documentation of evidence and reasoning for proposed choices and ensure this all flows as a prose story, combining context, diagnosis and recommended choices.

Once you have your story, if you are going to communicate it using slides, you want to create a storyboard. This is a translation of your story into a set of slide titles that when taken together, in succession, tell your story. That is, if you read the slide titles out loud, adding no further words (which is something you should actually do and not merely contemplate), you are telling all the key parts of the story.

Then, just as you did before when you created mock-ups of the diagnosis and hypotheses slides, you include on each dummy slide an outline of the evidence to be included that will support the "so what" in the slide title. From there and following the design and formatting guidelines in Chapter 4, you can create a full presentation recapping your diagnosis and recommending a set of choices that will form your strategy.

DELIVERABLES, CONCEPTS, ARC AND MEETINGS

Deliverables	• Recommended choices
	• Choices storyline
	• Choices storyboard
	• Choices presentation
Key concepts	• Situation-Complication-Resolution Framework
	• Storyline
	• Storyboard

Application of ARC	• Time is put aside to **rigorously** discuss different combinations of choices • A **collaborative** approach facilitates buy-in and grants everyone the opportunity to say which choices they would make and why • The set of choices taken together are **actionable** and are realistically sequenced.
Key meetings	Strategy design team: • Meeting 1 to debate choices and make recommendations. Meeting 2 (and 3 as needed) to review the story and storyboard including reading the slide titles of the storyboard out loud multiple times to refine them until they fully and accurately tell the story Steering committee: • Review recommendations on choices and come to final alignment on choices.

MAKING CHOICES

Let's suppose that you have identified three opportunities in three distinct markets, with the following characteristics:

Market 1: Reasonable demand for your existing products and services. Sales and marketing today has poor reach to this market.

Market 2: Strong demand. Needs are complex and not met by today's products and services. Will likely to need to quickly and continually innovate your products and services to keep these customers.

Market 3: Highest demand and projected growth rate but 50% risk of new regulations that could severely affect your ability to serve this market competitively.

These are all legitimate confirmed hypotheses. However, that does not mean that these become your strategy, they are just the set of possible strategic choices about where to play and what to offer.

In this example, you could choose to start in Market 1 with the least growth potential but where products and services match best, and build sales and marketing capability there. Or you could decide to start with Market 3 and make the most of the highest growth in the short term, knowing the opportunity may then disappear. In that case, you also then want to have another option to work on in the background which could compensate for the profit that might be lost in Market 3 if the new regulations do come into force. Sequencing matters when choosing between options; your first choice determines what else you can and should do.

One of the most important things to determine is how many strategic initiatives you can realistically deliver at any one time. This depends to some extent on your organization's size and bandwidth. If, for example, you are a small organization, it may be that your best chance of success would be to focus first on one strategic initiative and then wait to see if it is working before starting on another. But even if you are a large corporation, taking on lots of initiatives simultaneously rarely works. Better for a few strategic initiatives to succeed and grow from there.

To choose well, you need to remain objective and balance the potential impact of options with the practical requirements of delivering them tomorrow. Some years ago, I was asked to lead a division whose strategy I had written (prior to working in the division), so much for the theoretical calculations I had shared from the outside on how much gross margin percentage could be improved, now I had to do it. This only has to happen to you once, before you truly understand the difference between a plan that sounds marvellous in principle and one that can actually be delivered. Think about it—if you were fully responsible for delivery of the strategy, could you make it work? Step back and remind yourself of the original goal and question you articulated and reflect on which choice or choices will best fulfil this goal for your organization. And then choose.

Not making a choice is also a choice. So be just as explicit about what you don't do as what you are going to do. And yes you've guessed, it is all recorded in your *Discovery Document,* making it easy to build it on the strategy in future years. If you have transparency for the rationale behind choices made, when a change in the external environment occurs, which inevitably will happen at some point, you then have a rich set of information at your fingertips that enables you to quickly determine the implication of this change and what bearing it has on your strategy.

APPROACH TO DISCUSSING CHOICES

You want to give yourself, the strategy design team and all key stakeholders sufficient time to discuss the choices in front of you. A good approach is to circulate a final list of confirmed hypotheses in advance of your meetings, with a recap of the rationale for each plus an assessment of the potential impact and ease of implementation. You want to spell out numbers for impact and at least give a low, medium or high assessment for ease of implementation. You can share this as a table like the Prioritization Matrix shown at the end of Chapter 6.

Ask each participant to read this documentation in advance and confirm whether they agree with the prioritization—and if not, to bring to the meeting evidence and rationale for a different prioritization. Secondly, ask them to consider what a practical and complementary set of options would be and why—and be ready to discuss this at the meeting.

At the meeting, begin by reviewing the Prioritization Matrix for the options. Discuss these until you get alignment behind the prioritization. If you cannot agree on the prioritization, come to an agreement on what further evidence will be gathered and reviewed at the next meeting, where you can make the final prioritization decisions.

Once you have alignment on the prioritization, then you can discuss what would make a practical and complementary set of options. One approach is to ask each participant to share their thoughts on this so you get to hear from everyone. To avoid the anchoring bias, remind participants what this is and be sure not to start with the most senior person in the room, as once this happens people tend to unconsciously or consciously change what they were going to recommend to align with this person's views.

Often there is convergence on between one and four options that all agree should be part of the strategy. From there it becomes a discussion of what else is practical.

In instances where there are lots of options and quite different viewpoints, one approach is to map out different scenarios. For example, if you pursued options A, B, and D, what would that likely deliver? You can express this as a range, such as, if A, B and D perform really well then we'll deliver X and if they perform less well then we'll deliver Y. Also note the risks and how easy these would be to mitigate. Then the same question if you pursued B, C and E. You can try all combinations this way and as a team work through what each combination would likely deliver.

At this point, often the optimal set of options to pursue becomes self-evident. If that is not the case, revert back to evidence and consider what further evidence you would need to make a decision.

Let's play this out for ITC. Begin by identifying which combinations of opportunities can deliver the $8m to reach the $50m goal:

Confirmed hypothesis	Estimated impact	Ease of implementation
E & F. Modularized services & webshop	$5.2m	Low / Medium
A. Overseas sales teams	$2.4m	Medium
E. Modularized services without webshop	$2.1m	Medium
D. New contracts	$2.0m	High
F. Webshop without modularized services	$1.3m	Medium
C. Recycling	$1.2m	Medium / High

Options to deliver $8m: E & F, A, D = $9.6m and E & F, D, C = $8.4m

Insufficient: A, E, D, C = $7.7m and A, D, F, C = $6.9m

Figure 7.2: Table of options from which to choose

Next we need to consider each of these combinations in terms of ease of implementation. The output from this can be plotted on a Prioritization Matrix as we did for individual options, just now for the two possible sets of options:

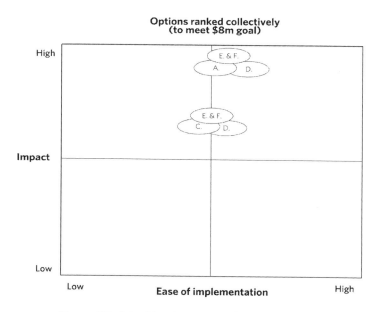

Figure 7.3: Prioritization matrix for opportunities
taken collectively

RECOMMENDED SET OF CHOICES

Once you have reviewed the collective impact and ease of implementation, it's time to decide. For ITC, only two sets of options are feasible: 1, a combination of E. & F., A. and D. or 2, a combination of E. & F., C. and D. The Prioritization Matrix indicates that option set 1, would deliver more impact and be a little easier to do. To confirm that this is the optimal combination of options—and this would especially be the case if you have one set of options that delivered more but was much harder to do—consider the following questions before making your final choice:

- Which provides a more balanced strategy?
- Which most reduces risk?
- Which is easier to resource?

Based on these criteria, then option set 1 is optimal. Let's suppose though that option set 2 were quite a bit easier to deliver than option set 1 and while it delivers less financially than option set 1 it still delivers enough to meet the goal. Then the heart of what you are considering, since in both cases three of the options are the same, is whether option C. Recycling, or option A. Overseas sales team is a better choice alongside E. Modularized services, F. Webshop and D. New contracts. One key factor here is that C. Recycling would provide additional services and we already have additional services in our choices set by way of E. Modularized services. More importantly, if we lose A. Overseas sales team, we reinforce ITC's dependence on US business and do not diversify risk. For balance, then with E, F and D selected, A. Overseas sales team is a more preferable addition than C. Recycling.

Initiative	Estimated impact	Ease of implementation
E. Modularized services	$3.9m	Medium
A. Overseas sales teams	$2.4m	Medium
D. New contracts	$2.0m	High
F. Webshop	$1.3m	Low / Medium
Collectively:	$9.6m	Medium

Make sure to list the details of how you got to your set of choices, including documenting any alternative scenarios you mapped out. That way, if questions are asked later about why certain decisions were made, you can easily provide background and evidence for these.

BRINGING IT ALL TOGETHER

With your recommended choices in place, you now need to review these choices with your steering commitee and achieve alignment.

A good way to do this is to use the Situation-Complication-Resolution (SCR) framework to recap the diagnosis and to present the recommended choices.

Figure 7.4: SCR Framework

The **situation provides the context**, the non-controversial facts. You can use the context you wrote on your question frame as the basis for this.

The **complication** describes your **diagnosis**, which covers the starting point, internal and external dynamics and their implications. Later it also includes how you will implement these choices.

The **resolution** then becomes the set of options which you recommend the organization should pursue and the rationale for choosing this particular set of options and not others.

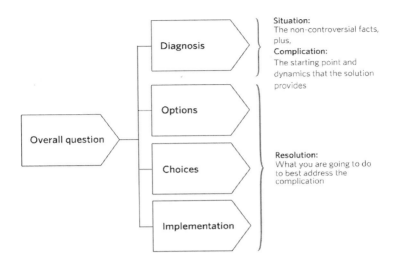

Figure 7.5: Relationship between Strategy in 5D question tree grouping and SCR

You use SCR to create a storyline in prose and use The Minto Pyramid Principle® to underpin the structure of each of the three sections. This allows all supporting evidence to be logically presented:

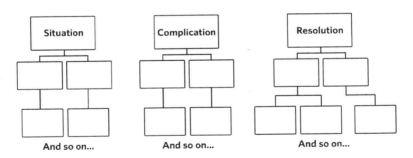

Figure 7.6: Layout of SCR in pyramid structure

You can lay out your storyline as outlined below, where the main bullets represent the key points in each of the Situation, Complication, Resolution sections and where the Resolution section is by far the most meaty. This should translate to how you spend your time; it is easy to spend time perfecting the Situation, however that section just needs to be good enough to level-set. Your focus needs to be on the Resolution as this is what requires discussion with your stakeholders and what you will need them to support.

SITUATION-COMPLICATION-RESOLUTION STORYLINE

Here is the SCR storyline structure in prose:

Situation

- Key context point
- Key context point

Complication

- Key diagnosis finding
  - Supporting evidence
- Key diagnosis finding
  - Supporting evidence

Resolution

- List of confirmed hypotheses
  - Supporting evidence by hypothesis, structured logically
- List of rejected hypotheses
  - Supporting evidence for rejection by hypothesis
- Impact and ease of implementation of confirmed hypothesis
  - Supporting evidence
- Possible combinations of confirmed hypotheses
  - Supporting evidence
- Recommended set of options
  - Supporting evidence

At the risk of stating the obvious, the storyline, told via SCR has to be grounded in what you have found. Occasionally on my strategy courses I see people at this stage write a storyline totally divorced from all their findings. You want to do quite the reverse—your storyline should include every important "so what" you have come up with in the course of the "develop" phase. I often use the *Discovery Document* as a checklist to make sure that I have included all the key "so whats."

Make sure that for all the "so whats" in the storyline you show the evidence that substantiates them. No more evidence than necessary of course, but no less either—don't let all your work gathering evidence go to waste. You want to also ensure that you include sources—both to add credibility and as a guide to someone who may read this much later—and that you show how each hypothesis was confirmed.

Once you have your "so whats'" and draft storyline in place, step back and reread the overall question. Ask yourself if your storyline addresses it and if there is anything still missing.

With the content of your storyline in place, now turn to how well it tells the story. You want your story to flow, so make sure that your key "so whats" and pieces of evidence are not just present, but logically linked and ordered in a way that naturally leads to the conclusion you have drawn. This will likely take rewriting the story multiple times, trying different orders and different wordings.

In my strategy courses I often tell participants that you want to write your story in such a way that a 10-year-old child could understand it. Your solution may be complex, but that doesn't mean that your communication of it needs to be complicated.

EXAMPLE STORYLINE

Following is an example storyline for ITC, which brings together parts of the story already written and provides the Resolution as far as proposed choices drawing on all the evidence in each Hypothesis Evidence Table:

Situation

- Over past three years, ITC has experienced 8% revenue growth, yielding $360m in 2015. Profitability has been flat in this same period and in 2015 was $38m
- A corporate plan estimated $42m profit for 2018, but this was rejected by the leadership team as insufficiently ambitious
- The CEO believes the next two years are critical to reinvigorating the company and kick-starting a growth trajectory and require reaching $50m profit.

Complication

- To meet $50m profit goal by 2018, ITC will need generate $8m beyond plan
  - Strategy in need of revision to encompass plans in services
  - Current projections fall short of three year profit target by $8m
  - Heavy reliance on USA for revenue and profit
  - Very heavy reliance on 17 customers with more than half of this revenue up for tender next three years
  - Competitor success coming from focus on specific customer groups with targeted offerings
  - Opportunity to create modularized services offer, particularly for medium and small businesses and to explore offering a cost-savings share model
  - Opportunity to extend existing end-of-life recycling offer.

Resolution

- Seven opportunities reviewed of which five confirmed and two rejected
  - Modularized services, webshop, new contracts, overseas sales teams and recycling were confirmed
  - Cost-savings share and slow-moving stock were rejected

- Modularized services: the creation of a modularized services offer, decoupling existing services packages, and with flexible à la carte choice of services, could yield $2.1m and $3.9m with a webshop in place
  - Nearly all smaller customers who were interviewed talked about the need for more flexibility to buy only the services they need and that having only packaged offerings restricted them from buying from ITC
  - Technology Partners has experienced significant growth following the route of modularized services and webshop
  - No new services design needed to modularize services—this is about marketing and pricing appropriately
  - No additional cost to implement beyond advertising and promotions budget—design can be done by in-house marketing team—estimated at $250k per year
  - With webshop in place, it's possible to double the number of small businesses and increase medium size by 20%. This would generate $4.15m profit per year less additional advertising costs of $250k, yielding $3.9m per year additional profits
  - Without a webshop, believe can increase small business by 30% and medium business by 10%, this would generate $2.1m per year additional profits

- Overseas sales team: by targeting existing customers with operations in Canada, Germany and the UK and with local sales teams in each of these countries, can increase profitability in all three markets by the end 2018
  - Established need for our services overseas with customers who trust us plus growth overall in these markets, suggesting opportunity also for new customers

- Of eight interviews with existing customers with operations in at least one of Canada, Germany and the UK, five said they would be seriously interested in doing business with us there, with same products/services and terms as in the US
  - All three are growing markets in services of at least 3% per year
  - If we could win just 20% of their business this would equate to a doubling of our profitability in those countries
  - No legal impediment to building business in either Canada, Germany and UK where already have businesses
  - Assume additional $0.8m per country profit per year by 2018

- New contracts: win three new contracts of at least $75m and $2m profit per year
  - Solid pipeline of over 20 prospects with contract size at least $75m
  - Sales team believe they can deliver at least 3 x $75m contracts
  - Historical profit on such contracts was 5% per year based on four year average = $75m /4 *0.04 = $0.93m per contract per year
  - Some new pressures on profitability which are estimated to reduce profits by up to 30%
  - Assume impact as $0.93m per contract per year, reduced by 30% to $0.66m per contract per year

- Webshop: by creating easy to navigate webshop, can increase small and medium business by 5% and conduct 80% of small and medium business and 40% of large business online, yielding $1.3m profit in 2018
  - Desire expressed in customer interviews to automate orders and to be able to place orders 24/7
  - Survey of customers suggests that 80% of small and medium business could go online within three years and 40% of large business
  - Significant growth of competitors with good webshops e.g. Technology Partners
  - Higher spend per small/medium customer of around 10% where good webshop in place

- Risk of losing small and medium customers altogether with no decent webshop
- Significant costs estimated at $2m to build, with build time of six months
- Assume will achieve higher spend per customer, could be 10% but estimate 5% to be prudent
- Need to start build asap to not lose opportunity

- Recycling: offer cradle-to-grave recycling modularized services for all hardware including that not purchased from ITC, and which includes filling of all associated paperwork to yield $1.2m additional profit per year by 2018
    - Recycling legislation in Europe and Canada already in place requiring all IT hardware to be recycled or appropriately disposed of
    - Recycling legislation arriving in US in 2018 which will create need for these services
    - Feedback from interviews with existing customers suggests this is something they just want solved—meaning requirement for one-stop shop for all recycling and related compliance services
    - Need to make process very simple and pain free to ensure adoption
    - Few offerings available today in USA
    - Assume can win $20k per year of recycling services with 50 customers by 2018 = $1m revenue per year
    - 10% of original value of approximately 40% equipment can be made by reselling it to metal traders
    - Revenue for metal traders, assuming 2018 original value $0.5m per customer, at 50 customers = $25m equipment, at 30% = $7.5m of equipment, sold at 10% = $0.75m
    - Cost to deliver services = 6 people x $100k average fully-loaded salary = $600k
    - Estimated profit per year by 2018 = $1m +$0.75m -$0.6m = $1.2m

- Cost-savings model: creating a cost-savings share model for managed services customers was also investigated but rejected
  - Without more concrete thoughts on how to manage risk, cash outlay required makes this is a non-starter
  - Customers like the concept because it reduces their risk
  - It's incredibly hard to determine what cost savings come as a result of this and what savings are the result of something else
  - Even when this can be measured, savings take time to transpire
  - Contrast this with large upfront costs for equipment, which would be a big drain on ITC cash flow
- Slow moving stock: selling off slow-moving stock more effectively was also investigated and rejected
  - Lots of online platforms where can sell slow-moving stock
  - Require up to the minute data and feeds to interface effectively with such platforms
  - Cost to buy technology for this likely to be in region of $2m
  - More detailed estimates suggest cost saving more like $0.3m per year as current selling off of slow-moving stock already includes some of this original $1m
- This provides two sets of options to meet the $8m goal
  - [Can show here table on possible combination of opportunities]
- Recommended set of choices are modularized services, webshop, new contracts and overseas sales team to yield $9.6m
  - [Show here recommended choices table]

KEY CONCEPT: WRITING A GREAT STORYLINE

What it is	What it is not
• Being structured and logical in the way you put the different elements of the story together and spending time to get this right	• Creating a story that is disconnected from or does not draw on "so whats".
• Using The Minto Pyramid Principle® and SCR as a way to structure	• Writing a story and then sticking to it, regardless of evidence to the contrary
• Testing whether the story would stand up as the answer to your question	• Omitting findings you do not like
	• Telling a story that does not answer the original question

THE STORYBOARD

The storyboard is the phase of translating your storyline into slides. This is exactly what we did for the dummy packs on diagnosis and hypotheses, but now we have our full storyline, hence the name "storyboard".

Just as in the dummy slides for the diagnosis and hypotheses, the key points of your storyline become the title of each new slide in the storyboard. The supporting evidence for the "so what" is the text or data that is on the body of the slide and listed in the supporting bullets of the storyline.

FROM STORYLINE TO STORYBOARD

You can write your storyboard on paper or directly in PowerPoint (although if you do the latter, resist the temptation to get into detail on particular slides at this stage).

When I first learned how to do this back in the late 1990s, we used to hand draw our storyboard presentation, just as you would if you were designing the illustrations or images for a motion picture or an animation. The slides would be designed in sequence so we could visualize the flow of the full presentation.

While it is rather old-fashioned, I find it much easier to do the storyboard on paper; I manually divide the page into boxes to represent slides and then add the slide titles. That way you can see everything at once in one place. You will inevitably change the title order and wording several times, so use either a pencil or have a few pieces of paper on hand the following are five steps I take:

1. Write, in order, the key points of your storyline as the titles of your slides. If you have spent time to make your storyline flow with pithy "so whats," then this exercise is very fast, you are simply translating the key points into slide titles.

2. Now read the slide titles aloud. Yes this may sound strange, but it doesn't work the same if you do it in your head.

   Once you have finished reading, do you feel that you have conveyed all your key messages? If there is anything missing, add it; anything superfluous, remove it.

   Ask yourself: do the titles flow? Are they in the right order? Play around with the order of slides until it really flows.

   Also do a quick practical check that you do not have too many slides for your meeting. A good rule of thumb is two minutes per slide. You can put additional slides into an appendix and refer to them if detailed questions come up.

   In the strategy courses I run, one of the coaching sessions begins with me asking you to come with your storyboard and for you to present to me, only articulating the titles of each slide, with no attention paid to any content that will go on the slides. Often I ask people to read the titles to me in succession two or three times. Because of this exercise, people regularly make small and sometimes big changes to clarify specific titles or to add or remove titles or slides, as well as changes to the order of the titles or slides, to make them flow more easily.

3. Once you are happy that your titles work, transfer the key supporting evidence for each "so what" onto the relevant slides. At this stage it is sufficient to write the evidence in text plus how you might present it rather than write it out in full.

4. Then, look at the design of the slides and the supporting evidence you are presenting on each and sketch out the best way to present the information.

5. Add subtitles and sources to each slide, as required.

On the following pages is an example storyboard for ITC based on the storyline with steps 1 to 3 above complete, but with more work to do to complete steps 4 and 5.

If you compare it with the storyline above you will notice some small differences where I needed to refine slide titles or needed to refine exactly what was on each slide for the logic and flow to work.

Goal set for $50m profit in 2018, up from $38m in 2015

- Over the past three years, ITC has experienced 8% revenue growth, yielding $360m in 2015. Profitability has been flat in this same period and in 2015 was $38m
- A corporate plan estimated $42m profit for 2018, but this was rejected by the leadership team as insufficiently ambitious
- The CEO believes the next two years are critical to reinvigorating the company and kick-starting a growth trajectory and require reaching $50m profit

To meet $50m profit goal by 2018, ITC will need to generate $8m beyond plan

- Strategy in need of revision to encompass plans in services
- Current projections fall short of three year profit target by $8m
- Heavy reliance on USA for revenue and profit
- Very heavy reliance on 17 customers with more than half of this revenue up for tender in the next three years
- Competitor success coming from focus on specific customer groups with targeted offerings
- Opportunity to create modularized services offer, particularly for medium and small businesses and to explore offering a cost-savings share model
- Opportunity to extend existing end-of-life recycling offer

> MAY WANT TO SPREAD INFORMATION OVER MULTIPLE SLIDES,
> WITH CHARTS FROM DIAGOSIS PACK

Seven opportunities reviewed of which five confirmed and two rejected

Confirmed hypotheses

- Modularized services
- Overseas sales team
- New contracts
- Webshop
- Recycling

Rejected hypotheses

- Cost savings share model
- Slow-moving stock

Modularized services alongside webshop could yield $3.9m incremental profit per year

- Nearly all smaller customers who were interviewed talked about the need for more flexibility to be able to buy only the services they need. Having only packaged offerings restricted them from buying from ITC
- Technology Partners has experienced significant growth following the route of modularized services and webshop
- No new services design needed to modularize services—this is about marketing and pricing appropriately
- No additional cost to implement beyond advertising/promotions budget—design can be done by in-house marketing team—estimated at $250k per year
- With webshop in place, it's possible to double the number of small businesses and increase medium size by 20%. This would generate $4.15m profit per year less additional advertising costs of $250k, yielding $3.9m per year additional profits
- Without a webshop, we believe we can increase small business by 30% and medium business by 10%, this would generate $2.1m per year additional profits

> RIGHT NOW THIS SLIDE IS A DATA DUMP. NEED TO PRESENT
> INFORMATION VISUALLY IN ONE OR MORE SLIDES

Overseas sales teams in Canada, Germany and the UK and target existing customers with operations in these three countries

- Established need for our services overseas with customers who trust us plus growth overall in these markets, suggesting opportunity also for new customers
- Of eight interviews with existing customers with operations in at least one of Canada, Germany and the UK, five said they would be seriously interested in doing business with us there, with the same products/services and terms as in the US
- All three are growing markets in services of at least 3% per year
- If we could win just 20% of their business this would equate to a doubling of our profitability in those countries
- No legal impediment to building business in either Canada, Germany and UK where already have businesses
- All three are growing markets in services of at least 3% per year
- Assume additional $0.8m per country profit per year by 2018

> RIGHT NOW THIS SLIDE IS A DATA DUMP. NEED TO PRESENT
> INFORMATION VISUALLY IN ONE OR MORE SLIDES

Win three new contracts of at least $75m by 2018 and generate $2m incremental profit per year

- Solid pipeline of over 20 prospects with contract size at least $75m
- Sales team believe they can deliver at least 3 x $75m contracts
- Historical profit on such contracts was 5% per year based on four year average = $75m /4 *0.04 = $0.93m per contract per year
- Some new pressures on profitability which are estimated to reduce profits by up to 30%
- Assume impact as $0.93m per contract per year, reduced by 30% to $0.66m per contract per year

> RIGHT NOW THIS SLIDE IS A DATA DUMP. NEED TO PRESENT
> INFORMATION VISUALLY IN ONE OR MORE SLIDES

Webshop: Create easy to navigate webshop

- Desire expressed in customer interviews to automate orders and to be able to place orders 24/7
- Survey of customers suggests that 80% of small and medium business could go online within three years and 40% of large business
- Significant growth of competitors with good webshops e.g. Technology Partners
- Higher spend per medium/small customer of around 10% where good webshop
- Risk of losing small and medium customers altogether with no decent webshop
- Significant costs estimated at $2m to build, with build time of six months
- Assume will achieve higher spend per customer, could be 10% but estimate 5% to be prudent
- Need to start build asap to not lose opportunity

> **RIGHT NOW THIS SLIDE IS A DATA DUMP. NEED TO PRESENT INFORMATION VISUALLY IN ONE OR MORE SLIDES**

Offer cradle to grave recycling services to deliver $1.2m incremental profit

- Recycling legislation in Europe and Canada already in place requiring all IT hardware to be recycled or appropriately disposed of
- Recycling legislation arriving in US in 2018 which will create need for these services
- Feedback from interviews with existing customers suggests this is something they just want solved—meaning requirement for one-stop shop for all recycling and related compliance services
- Need to make process very simple and pain-free to ensure adoption
- Few offerings available today in USA
- Assume can win $20k per year of recycling services with 50 customers by 2018 = $1m revenue per year
- 10% of original value of approximately 40% equipment can be made by reselling it to metal traders
- Revenue for metal traders, assuming 2018 original value $0.5m per customer, at 50 customers = $25m equipment, at 30% = $7.5m of equipment, sold at 10% = $0.75m
- Cost to deliver services = 6 people x $100k average fully-loaded salary = $600k
- Estimated profit per year by 2018 = $1m +$0.75m -$0.6m = $1.2m

> **RIGHT NOW THIS SLIDE IS A DATA DUMP. NEED TO PRESENT INFORMATION VISUALLY IN ONE OR MORE SLIDES**

Cost-savings share model hypothesis was rejected

- Without more concrete thoughts on how to manage risk, cash outlay required makes this a non-starter
- Customers like the concept because it reduces their risk
- It's incredibly hard to determine what cost savings come as a result of this and what savings are the result of something else
- Even when this can be measured, savings take time to transpire
- Contrast this with large upfront costs for equipment, which would be a big drain on ITC cash flow

> RIGHT NOW THIS SLIDE IS A DATA DUMP. NEED TO PRESENT INFORMATION VISUALLY IN ONE OR MORE SLIDES

Slow-moving stock hypothesis was also rejected

- Lots of online platforms where can sell slow-moving stock
- Require up to the minute data and feeds to interface effectively with such platforms
- Cost to buy technology for this likely to be in region of $2m
- More detailed estimates suggest cost saving more like $0.3m per year as current sell off of slow-moving stock already includes some of this original $1m

> RIGHT NOW THIS SLIDE IS A DATA DUMP. NEED TO PRESENT INFORMATION VISUALLY IN ONE OR MORE SLIDES

Of two sets of choices, recommended choices are

Confirmed hypothesis		Estimated impact	Ease of implementation
E & F.	Modularized services and webshop	$5.2m	Low/ Medium
A.	Overseas sales teams	$2.4m	Medium
E.	Modularized services without webshop	$2.1m	Medium
D.	New contracts	$2.0m	High
F.	Webshop without modularized Services	$1.3m	Medium
C.	Recycling	$1.2m	Medium/ High

Options to deliver $8m

E & F, A, D = $9.6m RECOMMENDED

E & F, D, C = $8.4m

Insufficient:

A, E, D, C = $7.7m

A, D, F, C = $6.9m

FROM STORYBOARD TO FULL CHOICES PRESENTATION

Once you have the presentation sketched out, turn your storyboard into formatted slides to give you the full presentation of choices.

For many of the slides in the example ITC storyboard above further work would need to be done to translate the text on the body of the slide into charts and visuals so that the presentation is not just lots of text.

Once this is done, do a final check to ensure that each slide has a clear title articulated as a "so what" and is articulating one message. Remember, you want to have drawn out all the inferences for the audience so they don't have to sit there and try and connect the dots themselves.

Don't forget to refer to the formatting guidelines in Chapter 4 and take time to make them look good, so your audience can focus on the content. One way to do that is to ensure clean, consistent and non-distracting formatting.

You may want to include an executive summary upfront, effectively your story written at the highest level over three to five bullets. This enables the audience to understand straight away what you will be sharing.

If we take the storyboard for ITC, we could add a title page and executive summary slide like the following:

Executive summary

- Corporate plan for 2018 of $42m profit leaves us $8m short of $50m goal

- Need to ensure can deliver plan through winning renewals and extending existing customers

- In addition, four initiatives can close the $8m gap:
  1. **Modularized Services:** Decoupling our existing services package and providing flexible à la carte choice of services

  2. **Webshop:** Create easy to navigate webshop

  3. **Recycling:** cradle-to-grave modularized recycling services for all hardware including any not purchased from ITC

  4. **New contracts beyond those assumed in plan:** Win three new contracts of at least $75m and $2m profit per year.

You should also check the wording and formatting on the storyboard. No doubt there will be a few changes, but essentially because you did the hard work to develop the storyline, from there the storyboard and choices presentation are easily derived.

CHOICES CHECKLIST

- Choices are made having reviewed all opportunities (confirmed hypotheses)
- The set of choices made are actionable and achieveable
- All key "so whats" and hypotheses are included
- Each paragraph begins with a major "so what"
- The key points of your story together form a clear and simple story, which you could tell a child
- The text of each paragraph supports its major "so what"
- All information is relevant and required to meet the objectives and address the audience's needs or concerns
- Knowing that on average it takes two minutes to present one slide, your number of slides fits the time you have for your presentation.

8

WRITING YOUR STRATEGY

"The ability to express an idea is well nigh as important as the idea itself."

Bernard Baruch

STRATEGY IN 5D

STEP	CHAPTERS
DEFINE	2. Defining your goal 3. Mapping the domain
DIAGNOSE	4. Diagnosing the situation
DEVELOP	5. Developing hypotheses 6. Testing hypotheses
DECIDE	7. Making choices 8. Writing your strategy 9. Communicating your strategy
DELIVER	10. Delivering your strategy

ACTIONABLE, RIGOROUS, COLLABORATIVE AT EVERY STEP (ARC)

KEY IDEAS

You have now determined your choices. With these choices made, so are the core tenets of your strategy determined. Since you have fostered buy-in for these choices, you can gracefully formulate them into a strategy in the knowledge that there is already support for it.

Contrast this with having designed a strategy involving little collaboration. You may have put in tremendous effort, developed fantastic, rigorously researched ideas and translated all of this into an elegantly written strategy, but if this is the first real glimpse that key stakeholders are getting of your ideas, then their focus is unlikely to be on how to make it work but on questioning your work and making it known where their own views differ.

Since you have been rigorously collaborative in your approach, you are now in a position where the strategy is a natural corollary of the buy-in and trust you have built. That means you can now focus on the next critical task: accurately documenting the strategy.

An effective strategy document provides:

- Clarity on the right things for the organization to do by overtly committing to paper what is part of the organization's strategy and what is not

- A set of measurable goals and timeframe for achieving these

- A guide for the work to be done and a framework for decision-making: staff at all levels of the organization should be able to read the strategy and determine whether their own or their team's actions are—or are not—in service of the strategy, and then continue or discontinue these actions accordingly

- A playbook for communication of the strategy for everyone in your organization and beyond. That means you need to be precise and informative as well as paint a goal and vision that inspires action.

As such, the strategy document (prose or slides) should contain:

1. **Mission and values:** either a restatement or a revised version of these for the organization based on the decisions made as part of the strategy

2. **A concise articulation of the strategy:** comprising where you are trying to get to, key actions you will take, what this will deliver and when. It can also be helpful to include a reminder of the current situation of the organization

3. **Detail on the choices that comprise the strategy:** including a recap of why each initiative was chosen, the expected financial impact and what investment, resources and any other enablers are required to deliver it

4. **Financial impact** of the strategy for revenue and profit, plus investment required and payback period(s)

Most of the above should essentially be a recap of what was previously discussed and agreed. Where there may be some new detail e.g., on financial projections, investments required or enablers, this should be highlighted when you present the strategy document to the steering committee.

To ensure that the strategy is actionable, the strategy document should also contain what is in effect a high-level implementation plan. This can be provided through sections on:

5. **Sequencing:** the timing and any interdependencies of the implementation of the choices

6. **Milestones:** the measures, quantitative and qualitative, you can put in place to swiftly assess success of new initiatives

7. **Governance:** who will be involved in

- delivering the initiatives
- overseeing and guiding the implementation of the strategy and deciding—once more is learned—whether changes to implementation or to strategy need to be made.

This section should also include what the forums for interaction will be and their cadence.

To best illustrate what a strategy document looks like, this chapter comprises a description of the different sections and how to apply this to your own strategy document, plus examples of each section for ITC.

Given the importance of the strategy document, it is imperative to get the wording precise, especially for the one to three sentence articulation of the strategy. So spend time on the wording, asking for feedback and revising it as often as needed to avoid future complications.

DELIVERABLES, CONCEPTS, ARC AND MEETINGS

Deliverable	• A written strategy document that can precisely articulate the strategy in no more than 20 slides or 10 pages. Do not discard the detail, just keep it as an appendix
Key concepts	• Sequencing • Milestones • Governance
Application of principles	• The written strategy includes a high-level implementation plan which is **actionable** • The **rigorous** thinking behind the strategy is reflected in how it is written. This means that all key insights that informed a decision are included • To ensure that the strategy is accurately and clearly represented, the approach to completing the strategy document is **collaborative.** Feedback is sought on the documentation and wording both from those who have been intensely involved and those who are new to the strategy
Key meetings	• Strategy design team: To review strategy document very carefully, before sending to steering committee. Can be done in part via meetings, part by email • Steering committee: Meeting to review strategy and sign off on it, including investment.

1. MISSION AND VALUES

In the "diagnose" phase, you reviewed the current mission statement and values. Now is the time to return to these and make changes to them if required, to ensure they encompass the new strategy. Often the mission and values are at a sufficiently high level that you don't need to change them, but in some cases you will need to revise or add to them. For example, suppose our strategy for ITC included a move into Asia, then the mission statement would need to be revised as follows:

Current ITC Mission: To be North America and Europe's partner of choice for provision of IT products and services.

Revised ITC Mission: To be North America, Europe and Asia's partner of choice for provision of IT products and services.

If you don't have a mission statement or you haven't written down your set of values then this a good time to create both of these documents. The best way to do this is collaboratively, by scheduling a specific strategy design team and stakeholder meeting to design and come up with a suggested mission and values that you can then share for review with the steering committee.

Typically I include the mission statement and values—along with any proposed revisions—as the first page (excluding title, contents, objectives etc.) of any strategy document. You can find ITC's in Chapter 4, as part of the diagosis slides.

2. CONCISE ARTICULATION OF THE STRATEGY

Your choices form your strategy and the key now is to express these in a clear way. Given that your strategy will be communicated many times, it is really important to get the wording right. This means testing the wording with different audiences, including those who have not been involved in the strategy to date, to remove any ambiguities or gaps.

Below is an articulation of ITC's strategy, including the articulation of starting and end points:

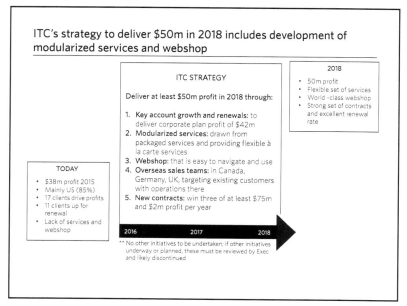

ITC's strategy to deliver $50m in 2018 includes development of modularized services and webshop

ITC STRATEGY

Deliver at least $50m profit in 2018 through:

1. **Key account growth and renewals:** to deliver corporate plan profit of $42m
2. **Modularized services:** drawn from packaged services and providing flexible à la carte services
3. **Webshop:** that is easy to navigate and use
4. **Overseas sales teams:** in Canada, Germany, UK, targeting existing customers with operations there
5. **New contracts:** win three of at least $75m and $2m profit per year

2018
• 50m profit
• Flexible set of services
• World-class webshop
• Strong set of contracts and excellent renewal rate

TODAY
• $38m profit 2015
• Mainly US (85%)
• 17 clients drive profits
• 11 clients up for renewal
• Lack of services and webshop

2016   2017   2018

** No other initiatives to be undertaken; if other initiatives underway or planned, these must be reviewed by Exec and likely discontinued

3. DETAIL ON THE CHOICES THAT COMPRISE THE STRATEGY

You then want to detail the choices in turn. For each you want to include:

• Description of the initiative
• Expected financial impact by year
• Investment required
• Enablers including:
  - Staff: what new and existing staff will be required
  - Skills: what skills, existing and those to be developed are required
  - Systems: both IT and operational processes required to be successful
  - Structure: any required organizational changes e.g. new reporting lines[12]

- Where appropriate, sales and marketing approach and key customer targets
- Whether what's required can be realized organically or will need to be delivered through acquisition, or a combination of the two
- Interdependencies.

The following are five slides describing each of the five initiatives for ITC, including what is required to deliver on the corporate plan:

Corporate plan: Win renewals to main contract bases and grow six key accounts

Name	2015 Profit	Due up next three years
Spectrum	4.1	Y
Handy Andys	2.9	Y
Bellview Hotels	2.1	Y
Johnsons and Co	1.9	N
Advantage	1.5	Y
Decorum	1.3	Y
Furniture World	1.2	N
Ashton Breweries	1.2	Y
Kirkton and Jameson	1.2	Y
Alexander Enterprises	1.1	N
Infinitum	1.1	Y
Generation X	1.1	N
Experience Holidays	1.1	N
Spotlight	1.1	Y
Excalibur	1.1	Y
Wainwright	1.0	N
Younger Games	1.0	Y
Total	26	
Contracts due next 3 years	11	

- **Key accounts:** Need to grow six contracts not up for renewal, by 9% per year

- **Renewals:** Need to increase overall revenue for those renewing by 3% per year, with no overall losses. Any contract losses need to be made up

Projected financials by year			
	2016	2017	2018
Revenue	$1.3m	$1.3m	$1.4m
Increamental Opex	$0	$0	$0
Profit	$1.3m	$1.3m	$1.4m
Key assumptions: Assume can use existing resources to deliver so no incremental cost			

Initiative owner TBC

Modularized services: Decouple our existing services packages and provide flexible à la carte choice of services

Projected financials by year				Key assumptions:
	2016	2017	2018	• Projected uptick of 20% in medium businesses and doubling in small businesses (to 2% overall)
Revenue	$0.2	$1.5m	$4.15m	
Incremental opex	$0.27	$0.26	$0.25m	• Design can be done by in-house marketing team. Therefore additional costs are:
Profit (pre depreciation)	($0.07)	$1.2m	$3.9m	- Advertising/promotions budget at $250k per year; - Training outside normal budget: 2015: $20k, 2016: $10k, 2017: $0k
Capex	$0k	$0k	$0k	• Revenue dependent on creation of webshop by latest end Q1 2017

Staff	Skill	System	Structure
• Second two members of services design team to work on this full time • No new recruits but need advertising budget	• Develop skills in innovation and translating customer needs into services through training	• No new systems required to support • Dependent on webshop to market	• Create modularized services design Lead, reporting into services director

Initiative owner TBC

Webshop: Create easy to navigate webshop

Projected financial by year				Key assumptions:
	2016	2017	2018	• Build will cost $2m and can be finished by end Q1 2017 (build time six months but need to select provider and plan what really want), plus expect some slippage on six months timeframe)
Incremental Revenue	$0	$0.4m	$1.3m	
Opex	$0	$0.3m	$0.3m	
Cost savings	$0	$0.15m	$0.3m	
Profit (pre depreciation)	$0m	$0.3m	$1.3m	• To maintain webshop need three system administrators at cost of $75k each
Capex	$2m			• Use existing call center team to handle calls and emails from webshop customers • Systems running costs are $100k per year

Initiative owner TBC

Overseas sales teams: Create in Canada, Germany and UK and target existing customers with operations in these countries

Projected financials by year					Key assumptions:
	2015 (actuals)	2016	2017	2018	
Revenue • Canada • Germany • UK	$29m $16m $18m	$34m $19m $23m	$40m $25m $28m	$46m $31m $34m	• Will build organically; no business we could buy in these countries gives us what we need • Assume one head of business per country, $250k fully loaded • Assume start with six sales staff per region, fully loaded cost of $120k or 100k each, increasing to 10 and then 12 people
TOTAL REVENUE	$63m	$76m	$93m	$111m	• Assume four admin staff per country at fully loaded $75k each, rising to eight and then nine
Gross margin (12%)	$7.6m	$9.1m	$11.2m	$13.3m	• Assume office leasing budget of $150k per year, doubling
Operating costs today	$3m	$3m	$3m	$3m	• Assume travel and entertainment budget of further $250k per country per year
Incremental operating cost	n/a	$1.7m	$3m	$3.4m	• Assume IT equipment, licenses and support $50k per year
Total profit	$4.5m	$4.4m	$5.2m	$6.9m	• No Capex
Incremental profit	n/a	($0.01m)	$0.6m	$2.4m	(Full breakdown of costs in appendix)

Initiative owner TBC

New contracts: Win three new contracts of at least $75m and $2m profit per year

- Currently pursuing eight potential new contracts
- Will be more contracts issued over next three years
- Need to win at least one big one of $75m per year
- We currently have seven that are more than $75m in size
- Should recruit one expert bid writer at $120k fully loaded per year
- Should introduce rigorous bid review process for leadership team and others to contribute to bid while it is being written and to rehearse for pitches

Initiative owner TBC

4. Financial impact

Here you want to show a complete picture of the financial impact of the strategy, both overall and detailed by initiative.

Five key initiatives, including corporate plan, to deliver additional $9.6m profit

Initiative	Estimated impact	Ease of implementation
1. Deliver corporate plan through key account growth and strong renewals	$4.0m	Medium
2. Modularized services	$3.9m	Medium
3. Overseas sales teams	$2.4m	Medium
4. New contracts	$2.0m	High
5. Webshop	$1.3m	Low/Medium
Collectively:	$9.6m	Medium

A good way to represent the summary financial information visually is in a waterfall chart that maps the profit today against desired profit and shows what each initiative will contribute financially to meeting that goal.

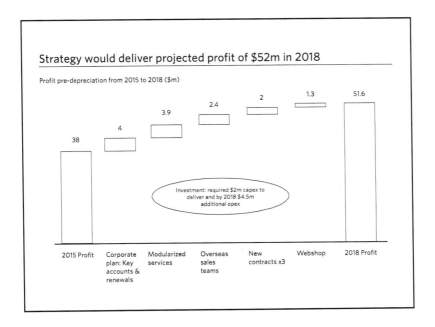

5. Sequencing

You want to think about the timing for rolling out each initiative in a way that reflects any interdependencies and that is also a realistic number of things to be roll out at any one point in time, especially where multiple initiatives may draw on the same resource.

You want to break each initiative down into different steps of what needs to be delivered and list each of these in order (with some quite possibly being in parallel) along with timing for each.

A good way to represent this visually is in a Gantt chart as introduced in Chapter 4 and as in the example following:

The five initiatives would be phased over three years

		2016				2017				2018			
		Q1	Q2	Q3	Q4	Q1	Q2	Q3	Q4	Q1	Q2	Q3	Q4
1. Key account growth and renewals: Deliver planned key account growth and contract renewals to provide corporate plan profit of $42m	Ensure sales teams understand the importance of meeting these goals	■											
	Put in place new bid review procedures; renewals & new contracts		■										
	Ongoing delivery of goals				■				■				■
2. Modularized services: Decoupling our existing services packages and provide flexible à la carte choice of services	Identify which services should be decoupled and sold à la carte		■										
	Determine pricing for these services			■									
	Design marketing and copy for website				■								
	Hire marketing agency to run promotion campaign					■							
	Conduct customer interviews for feedback and to identify needs & trends							■					
3. Webshop: Developing easy to navigate webshop	Determine key features of webshop	■											
	Write spec		■										
	Have beauty parade of providers and select one			■									
	Build				■	■							
	Ongoing management and maintenance							■				■	
4. Overseas sales teams: in Canada, Germany, UK, targeting existing customers with operations there	Recruit country heads for each country	■											
	Recruit sales teams; first wave		■										
	Recruit admin staff; first wave		■										
	Find premises and set up logistics			■									
	Recruit sales teams; second wave				■								
	Recruit admin staff; second wave				■								
	Recruit sales teams; third wave							■					
5. New contracts beyond those assumed in plan: Win three new contracts of at least $.75m and $2m profit per year	Recruit new bid manager	■											
	Make pipeline system more rigorous		■										
	Put in place pipeline reviews			■									
	Ensure win at least one contract per year				■				■				■

6. Milestones

For each initiative you want to define upfront milestones for each year of the strategy. These include meeting the financial goals, but beyond that also other goals around development and launch of new products or services and hiring of new staff or development of new skills.

2016 milestones have been set for each initiative

Initiative	2016 overall
1. Corporate plan: key account growth & strong renewals	• $1.3m incremental profit • Growth in at least two of six targeted key accounts • Renewal of six accounts and to contract base equivalent to at least previous total
2. Modularized services	• New services designed and launched • Advertising program in place to extend into 2017 • Breakeven financially • Do no exceed $300k incremental costs • On course to make $1.2m incremental profit in 2017
3. Overseas sales team	• One new head of business in place in each Canada, Germany and UK • Six new sales staff in each of three countries • Four new admin staff in each of three countries • Breakeven financially • Do no exceed $300k incremental costs • On course to make $0.6m incremental profit in 2017
4. New contracts	• Win at least one new contract of at least $75m • Have in place one new expert bid writer • Rigorous bid review process in place for leadership team and others to contribute to bid while it is being written and to rehearse for pitches
5. Webshop	• Webshop at least 80% and ready to launch in Q1 2017 • Full build costs not to exceed $2m

Initiative owner TBC

7. Governance

It is critical to put in place ways to manage and review progress in implementing the initiatives. No doubt, things that you hadn't thought of will come up or things won't turn out how you expected and it is important to be able to have others around to best advise your course of action.

Good governance also holds people to account. You have not made all this effort to have a strategy for it not to happen. Any individual or groups involved in governance should ensure that milestones are being met and if they are not, enquire why they are not being met and what needs to be done in response.

Finally, good governance should provide a forum for learning: if you can understand what has worked well and why, and what has worked less well and why, then everyone gains important lessons not just for the remaining implementation but also for all sorts of other situations that occur in the future.

For this to be effective, it requires an environment that allows those involved in implementation to equally share mistakes and successes and for them to be received in an open, curious way, rather than with any sense of only wanting to hear good news, or using the sharing of mistakes as a way to reprimand someone. As soon as that happens just once, you can forget about hearing honest feedback. Not that someone should never be reprimanded, but this cannot take place in a meeting where you are inviting people to share openly.

There are various ways in which to provide the desired governance. One approach can be to use the steering committee that designed the strategy as an oversight committee, who can help you keep on track by meeting ever quarter.

You may also want to have a delivery office who take on a more formal responsibility to governance and delivery. We will talk more about this in Chapter 10.

Whether you have a delivery office or not, you are likely to want an operational level committee. They should meet once a month at least, if possible more often.

Make sure you create a culture of accountability for the meetings. For example, there should be a clear set of actions—with tasks delegated to owners—coming out of each operational committee. This should be systematically reviewed at the following meeting and there should be no excuses for not having completed actions (or else the meeting risks becoming a talking shop rather than a vehicle for getting things done).

> **Proposed governance includes reviewing program progress each month and overall progress on strategy with steering committee quarterly**
>
> | | Purpose | Frequency |
> |---|---|---|
> | **Strategy steering committee** | • Review progress against milestones
• Discuss any big changes / surprises to what expected
• Agree any significant change to plan | • Quarterly
• Papers submitted in advance |
> | **Project team review** | • Review progress against milestones
• Review detailed operations on each initiative, with all initiative owners to present
• Discuss any big changes / surprises to what expected
• Agree any minor changes; any minor changes should be recommended to strategy steering committee for approval (no need to wait for meet; email request or set up extra specific meeting) | • Monthly |

At this stage, you also want to start thinking about owners for each of the key initiatives underpinning your strategy, plus owners for any functional areas like IT or HR that span across multiple initiatives. We will return to this in Chapter 10.

STRATEGY DOCUMENT CHECKLIST

The strategy document includes:

- A clear and concise articulation of the initiatives that make up the strategy
- Sufficient detail on each initiative to know financial projections and key enablers
- The financial goals and expected impact
- The sequencing and interdependencies of the initiatives
- How progress will be reviewed and managed (milestones and governance).

9

COMMUNICATING YOUR STRATEGY

"Communication is about getting others to adopt your point of view, to help them understand why you're excited. If all you want to do is create a file of facts and figures, then cancel the meeting and send in a report."

Seth Godin

STRATEGY IN 5D

STEP	CHAPTERS
DEFINE	2. Defining your goal 3. Mapping the domain
DIAGNOSE	4. Diagnosing the situation
DEVELOP	5. Developing hypotheses 6. Testing hypotheses
DECIDE	7. Making choices 8. Writing your strategy 9. Communicating your strategy
DELIVER	10. Delivering your strategy

ACTIONABLE, RIGOROUS, COLLABORATIVE AT EVERY STEP (ARC)

KEY IDEAS

You have done a tremendous amount of work to get here. Now make sure the communication of your strategy goes well.

How well you communicate affects the level of support for the strategy and people's willingness to do the hard work required to put it into practice.

Simply put, if you can't get the people who need to deliver the strategy on your side, then you are going to find it difficult to deliver the strategy. On a more personal level, it also affects how you and your work are perceived, particularly by those who don't know you well.

I won't spend time here discussing all the presentation related soft skills, such as body language and use of the voice—there are plenty of books on this. Our focus is on the preparation, objectives and content of the presentation and how to best navigate on the day.

You are likely to have three core audiences to address with your strategy: the steering committee, the wider staff and your external audience including investors, customers and suppliers.

For every audience you want to define what you want the outcome of the meeting to be, and whether that means you will need to inform your audience, engage them in the strategy or whether you actually want to discuss it with them. (This is analogous to how you prepare for a meeting, as we discussed in Chapter 2.)

With the steering committee you are sharing the strategy based on choices they have already agreed with. You will likely have added more detail on the financials, sequencing, milestone and governance and you want there to be time to discuss these and to genuinely make changes as a result.

With staff, you want to first think about whether to segment them into groups for communication purposes. For example, you may want to separate those who are going to be involved in implementing the strategy from those who will not be directly involved but should be aware of their organization's plan. Or you may want to segment your audience by seniority, with those who are middle or senior managers briefed in advance of a presentation to all staff so that they are prepared to answer questions from their staff.

In terms of the purpose of presenting to staff, you are essentially informing them of the strategy. If there are any staff that you want to share the strategy with and get feedback from, then that needs to happen prior to going to the steering committee meeting in which the strategy document is signed off on. This really is about the intent and tone you set for the presentation: if you actively want input say so. If you are at a stage where you are no longer actively looking for input, be genuinely receptive to it, but there is no need to make any promises to incorporate it.

While your intent and tone is one of informing people about the strategy, you may actively want to encourage input on how it will be delivered. This will likely give you a richer set of ideas and help with buy-in for the hard work of implementation ahead.

With any external audience at this stage your task will be to inform in a way that shows relevance to their needs. As with staff, if you want views from colleagues external to the organization then that needs to happen earlier during the "discovery" phase.

With your audiences and objectives in place, add in the audience's needs and then consider how to tailor the strategy document—your base presentation—to meet these needs.

To bring all this together, you want to create a strategy launch communications plan that also includes timing of the meetings. You should do this collaboratively with the strategy design team and with input from stakeholders to ensure no audience is missed and any potentially tricky meetings can be well thought through. There is often sequencing as to who should come first. You should also think about if you want the same person/people to present or if you will vary that based on the audience. The location of meetings also matters, for example it sends a different message if people to come to you, versus if you go to them.

A key skill, no matter who your audience, is to keep your objectives front and center in your mind, both while preparing the presentation and during delivery. Then, regardless of surprises—be it that you receive a set of unexpected questions that take you off course— you can tailor your response in a way that still enables you to meet your objectives.

Here, it is critical to have or develop a feel for time. You want to know how long each section of the presentation takes. Then, if for example, your time is halved, you can very quickly work out what to drop and what to keep. You also know how much time to allow for questioning that maybe a little off topic and when it is time to politely move on.

You also want to think about your environment, about the setting in which you will be presenting, as it makes a big difference to how people feel and behave. You don't always have a choice in this but when you do, you want to think about the type of room and layout that will best create the atmosphere you want. Also, be sure to have the technology and props you need. For example, projector, whiteboard, flipcharts, video conferencing, and if you are not familiar with the room, test it all works beforehand. There is nothing worse than having done all this work only to be hampered in your delivery by technology not working as it should.

Really, this phase prior to delivering your presentation is about being as prepared as you can be.

DELIVERABLES, CONCEPTS, ARC AND MEETINGS

Deliverables	• Strategy presentation to target audiences
Key concepts	• Communications plan for strategy launch
Application of principles (examples)	• The comms plan is **actionable** with clear owners and timing • The comms plan is **rigorously** thought through, with approaches tailored to each audience • The comms plan is created and reviewed **collaboratively** to ensure optimal messaging and no audience overlooked

Key meetings	Strategy design team:
	• Need to conduct meetings to—
	  – Create comms plan for strategy launch
	  – Deliver presentation
	Steering committee
	• meet to —
	  – Review comms plan for strategy launch
	  – Discuss feedback from presentations
	  – Celebrate launch with strategy design team

DEVELOPING COMMS PLAN FOR STRATEGY LAUNCH

The comms plan for sharing your strategy should include ten elements:

1. **Audience:** who you are communicating to

2. **Purpose:** of communicating to them including whether to inform, engage or discuss

3. **Desired outcomes:** what you want the audience to know, feel and do as a result

4. **Audience needs:** what the audience will be looking to have addressed

5. **Medium:** how communication will take place. For example, in person with handouts, in person with a presentation on screen, via a webcast or on a conference call.

6. **Number of meetings:** to be able to reach the audience

7. **Material:** what will be used and what will be provided to the audience, plus any pre-reading required. Consider what tweaks you require to your base presentation and also the impact of your medium. For example, you can typically include a little more detail on slides that are handouts versus slides that will only be presented on screen

8. **Location:** where the communication will occur

9. **Presenter(s):** who will deliver it

10. **Timing:** when it will occur.

You also want to think about how you can support the above plan, for example, by posting material on the company intranet or posting flyers in offices that would reinforce messages after meetings.

The plan for communicating the strategy is, of course, only the start of the communications required for successful delivery of the strategy. As part of the implementation plan, you will need to have a communications workstream and determine how you will best update people on progress and keep them engaged long-term.

An example Strategy Launch Comms Plan for ITC follows on the next page:

Audience	Purpose	Desired outcomes	Audience needs	Medium	# meetings	Location(s)	Presenter(s)	Material	Timing
Steering committee	• Share final strategy with new details on finances and implementation • Highlight and get feedback on these new additions • Get buy-in for strategy and its dissemination	• Steering committee fully aligned and supportive • Avoid rediscussing any areas already agreed • Steering committee offer help to communicate strategy	• See a strategy they believe will work • Feel that any concerns or questions are addressed	• In person meeting	• 1	• Head office	• Strategy team leader; members on design team as per areas of strategy they have worked on	• Strategy document with full appendices • Strategy document circulated in advance; print out available at meeting	• Mar 7th
Top 50 managers group	• Share strategy • Impart importance of their roles to deliver it • Signal that need their input for implementation detail • Hear any concerns	• Understanding of the strategy • Support and enthusiasm for the strategy • Readiness to be able to talk to staff about it	• Understand organization's direction • Know what strategy means for their jobs and what is expected of them	• In person meeting	• 1	• Head office	• CEO • Strategy design team leader	• Strategy document with full appendices • Print out of strategy document; no pre-read	• Mar 14th

Audience	Purpose	Desired outcomes	Audience needs	Medium	# meetings	Location(s)	Presenter(s)	Material	Timing
All staff	• Share strategy • Impart how pivotal many of their roles are in delivering it • Hear any concerns	• Understanding of the strategy • Support and enthusiasm for the strategy	• To understand whether their job is still safe (usual concern whenever do strategy review) • To understand where their roles will change • To understand where the organization is going	• In person meetings	• 6	• Roadshow around country in following six locations: - San Francisco, New York, Miami, Austin, Chicago, Los Angeles	• CEO • Strategy design team leader • Local most senior staff member	• Strategy document, no appendices • Printed out summary of strategy (not full document); no pre-read	• Mar 15th - Mar 18th

Audience	Purpose	Desired outcomes	Audience needs	Medium	Number of meetings	Location(s)	Presenter(s)	Material	Timing
Investors	• To get them excited about next phase of growth for the organization	• Feel positive about their investment • More likely to increase investment having heard the strategy	• To know their money is in good hands and is being wisely used	• In person meeting • Webcast	• 1 • 1	• New York • n/a	• CEO; CFO • CEO; CFO	• Strategy document, no appendices • Printed out summary of strategy no pre-read	• Mar 21 • Mar 24
20 key accounts, plus any others inter-viewed	• Share benefits that will come to them as a result of the strategy e.g. new services • Thank them for any input provided	• Keen to buy new services • Tell others about the new offerings	• To know how the strategy will benefit them	• Mix of in person, webcast and conference calls	• >20	• Various but where in person ideally at customer site	• Lead account manager, plus project team members as available; CEO or BU heads may attend for largest customers	• Strategy document, no appendices • Emailed summary of new services expected; no pre-read	• April various

Audience	Purpose	Desired outcomes	Audience needs	Medium	Number of meetings	Location(s)	Presenter(s)	Material	Timing
Four key suppliers plus any other interviews	• Share needs of suppliers arising from strategy • Thank them for any input provided	• Suppliers to think about how they work with ITC today and whether any changes required as a result of the strategy	• Understand whether their services are still needed and if any changes as a result of the strategy	• Mix of in person, webcast and conference calls	• >4	• Various, but where in person ideally at customer site	• Lead procurer, plus project team members as available	• Strategy document, no appendices • Emailed summary of the strategy; no pre-read	• April various

PREPARING FOR EACH PRESENTATION

One of the most important things you can do when writing and giving a presentation is to put yourself in the shoes of the audience. This will give you invaluable perspective and alert you to audience needs and concerns that may arise. It also helps tailor the precise language and tone of your presentation.

You should do this specifically for each audience and use what you see as way to preempt likely questions and concerns. I often make a list of the questions I expect and then make notes on the answer I would give.

Other things to consider as you prepare:

- **Be explicit about the purpose of the presentation upfront,** in the invite to the meeting and again at the begin of the meeting to frame it

- **Plan your presentation in carefully timed blocks**, including time for questions and discussion—and be realistic about how long things will take

- **Do a final review of your slides for typos and for superfluous words**. Every word counts, so if a word or phrase is not adding anything, cut it out

- **Do a dry-run,** even if only to yourself. Do it in the format you will be presenting, so if it will be on screen, practice the presentation on screen, not with a print out

- **Check any equipment you will be using before the day of the presentation.** This may sound trivial, but I have seen equipment not working on the day enough times and it can have devastating effects. It will at the very least unnerve you and at worst mean that people cannot actually see

- **Know your material so well that you no longer really need your slides.** That way, you are likely to be more natural and fluid in your responses and much less likely to read verbatim from your slides

- **Set up a pre meeting** where you are particularly concerned about an audience member's response or where it is critical to have their support at the presentation. Use it to run through the presentation and be able to address any concerns privately

- **Circulate any helpful pre-reading material**. Choose pre-reading material carefully, you want the audience to be well-informed and able to think prior to the meeting, but not to cause misinterpretation and unhelpful chit-chat and rumor about what it means. When communicating a new strategy to an audience who have not been involved in its design, usually a pre-read does not make sense since it would more likely lead to more questions and risk of misinterpretation prior to the presentation.

DELIVERING THE PRESENTATION

It's the day of one of your presentations. Here are a few important things to do during the presentation:

- **Get yourself comfortable.** Don't rush to start. Be poised. Get a feel for the room and the audience. They are here to listen to you, and what you have to say is important

- **Start with a proper introduction** and context to get everyone on the same page. You know why you are there, but the audience, in one of many meetings in their day, may not immediately recall

- **Avoid talking too fast,** which is easy to do if you are nervous. I sometimes write in the margins of my slides "don't talk too fast" as a reminder. You can also tell someone in the room about this and ask them to signal if you are talking too fast

- **Find a friend** and do so fast, meaning as you refer to something that you know is important to one of the audience members, verbally acknowledge the audience member and their viewpoint at the same time. For example, "Jane, I know you raised the need to balance strategy with more operations overseas and you'll see that we have incorporated this as an important part of the strategy." This will help engage the person and bring you an early ally. You can repeat this a few times with different people especially if someone looks unengaged. It is a great way to bring them into the presentation

- **Be sure to highlight the key message** of each slide and guide the audience through what they are looking at with each slide, but avoid reading verbatim. For example, "On the left you can see a bar chart showing profitability in Germany over the past three years. This shows stagnation in our profitability caused by... On the right you have quotes from some of our US customers who have operations in Germany but who we don't serve today. Of note is..."

- **Pre-empt likely questions or objections** to slides as you describe them. Suppose there have been concerns as to how to address recent customer feedback. You can pre-empt a lot of discussion by making a statement such as: "You might be wondering how this will help address the recent customer feedback we received. Well..." and then go on to explain how the strategy does this

- **Add color to your slides** with examples or anecdotes. I sometimes add Post-It® notes with examples on specific slides so I remember to talk about those examples when I am on the earmarked slide

- **Be aware of the audience's body language** as this can reveal how much they are following and engaged

- **Allow space to receive comments or questions from the audience.** Remember, people are much more likely to be supportive if they feel their points are acknowledged and addressed

- **Verbally check in with the audience every few slides,** asking if there are any questions on what has been presented so far. This is especially important if you are not getting many comments or questions

- **State the slide number you are on** every couple of slides if you have people listening or watching remotely.

AVOIDING DERAILMENT

What to do if the audience starts asking lots of questions that take you off topic? This a big concern for many presenters. Do you answer them at the risk of not getting through your material, or do you move on, and when?

My advice would be to allow a few questions like this. If they continue, and you can see that you are going to run out of time, I suggest acknowledging the person and their questions and asking if you can continue another time. For example, "I'd love to discuss more of your questions, but I am conscious that we only have X minutes remaining. If we continue I am concerned that we won't get through the rest of the presentation which I think has some important ideas we should cover today. Would it be okay if we pause on the questions for this session and agree a follow-up session to discuss them in depth as soon as possible?"

UNEXPECTED QUESTIONS

I am also often asked what to do if, despite good preparation, you are asked a question you are not prepared for and do not know the answer to.

Should you get flustered, then first re-center yourself and take a couple of breaths before responding. Then, flustered or not, I do not advise trying to piece together an answer if you really don't know it. Better to acknowledge that it's an important question and that you'd like to think about it first or that you need to check a couple of pieces of information before responding. Then promise to get back to the person with the answer fast. Provide a timeframe for this and make sure you do follow-up in that timeframe. There is rarely anything that needs to absolutely be answered immediately. So in almost all cases, it is much better to have the right answer later than to have a guess in the moment.

COMMUNICATIONS CHECKLIST

- Communications plan is in place with all ten elements included

- You have a good feel for your audience and their needs and concerns before you get in the room

- You spent time to prepare for presentations beyond writing slides, for example, checking out the room and planning the time allotted per section of the presentation

- You calibrate the storyline, insights and presentation to the audience, varying level of detail, complexity and length depending on the audience type and needs

- You have done a timed dry-run

- You feel confident about what you will be presenting.

10

DELIVERING YOUR STRATEGY

"Without strategy, execution is aimless.
Without execution, strategy is useless."

Morris Chang

STRATEGY IN 5D

STEP	CHAPTERS
DEFINE	2. Defining your goal 3. Mapping the domain
DIAGNOSE	4. Diagnosing the situation
DEVELOP	5. Developing hypotheses 6. Testing hypotheses
DECIDE	7. Making choices 8. Writing your strategy 9. Communicating your strategy
DELIVER	10. Delivering your strategy

ACTIONABLE, RIGOROUS, COLLABORATIVE AT EVERY STEP (ARC)

KEY IDEAS

You have a strategy in place and it has been communicated to all relevant parties. But if you can't deliver it, then it is not worth the paper it is written on.

The transition from finalized choices, to delivery is the most challenging part, where things can easily go wrong. Countless times I have heard stories of beautiful, thought through strategy documents never leaving the manager's desk drawer. The people in charge of delivering the strategy are often, quite understandably, not the same people who designed it. If good practice has been followed, these same people will have already provided input on the design of the strategy.

Rigorously transferred knowledge to the strategy delivery owners is critical. Otherwise the change in day-to-day management from design to delivery can lead to thinking being lost, actions falling through the cracks or worse still, the strategy just not happening.

This transition also reminds us why ARC is such an important set of principles:
- If the designers of the strategy did not make the strategy **actionable**, then there will certainly be a hiatus and possibly a permanent stop.
- If the documented strategy is not **rigorous**, then the gaps may lead to mistakes and oversights in delivery.
- Without **collaborative** input from both a good set of stakeholders and from the key people who will deliver, then there will not be enough support from the organization's leaders to continue to support the strategy in tougher times (much easier to later say "I never agreed with the strategy in the first place" if you weren't collaboratively engaged in its development).

Nor will it be so easy to get buy-in from those who need to deliver it. They are more likely to be defensive about plans imposed on them, versus plans they were collaboratively involved in developing.

Start with assigning owners for each of the initiatives. If your initiatives rely heavily on functions such as IT, you may also need functional lead(s) who are responsible for their functional area as required for each initiative. Then work closely with all the initiative owners to ensure they understand the strategy and what is expected of them, and have what they need to succeed.

You may want to set up a delivery office to oversee the delivery of the strategy, particularly if there are many different parts of the organization involved in delivering the strategy. This ensures dedicated expertise on the "how to" and on the running of the governance to deliver the strategy, plus ensures sharing of best practices between initiatives.

The role of the delivery office can range from lighter touch co-ordination of workstreams (delivery coordinator) to a role that helps to plan and deliver the implementation (delivery director) or something in the middle (delivery manager). In the latter case, this more senior role is heavily involved in holding people to account for delivering the strategy and may therefore require initiative owners to have a dotted reporting line to the delivery director / manager as well as the reporting line to their current manager.

To aid the transition, there also needs to be a swift translation of the strategy into a detailed implementation plan, divided into workstreams. This should include one workstream for each initiative, one for each of the key functional areas such as IT and HR, and one for each of governance and communication.

Each owner should develop the detail on his or her initiative, with functional leads and—where they exist—the delivery team completing the governance workstream. This group of owners should then come together to collaboratively review what all this adds up to and make changes and fill any gaps to ensure coherence.

Unlike the strategy document, which once written is fixed (bar any revisions required due to significant changes in circumstances), think of the implementation plan as a dynamic, living document which should be regularly updated to document what has been done, what has been learned and what this all means when translated into future plans.

I cannot emphasize enough the importance of being willing to try things and make mistakes—and of course, learn from them. However much we put the best brains to work when designing a strategy, no-one can forsee every instance or predict every change that makes subtle or not so subtle refinements to the strategy necessary.

Effective governance not only ensures progress stays on track but also facilitates this culture of testing and piloting of each initiative, where changes to delivery are decided swiftly based on what is learned, and the final delivery is well honed and refined.

This chapter does not claim to comprehensively cover how to deliver a strategy—that would take another book—but it provides some important concepts and principles to incorporate into your delivery so you can realize your goal.

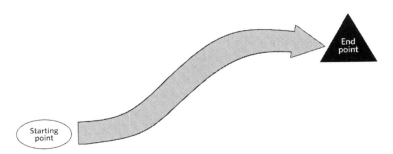

Delivery being refined and honed as more is learned.

Figure 10.1: Navigating delivery to the desired end point

DELIVERABLES, CONCEPTS, ARC AND MEETINGS

Deliverables	• Implementation plan
Key concepts	• Delivery office • Piloting
Application of principles (examples)	The implementation plan is: • **actionable** with clear, unambiguous steps to be taken that any good manager would be able to follow • **rigorous** with no gaps. Where you don't know what to do yet, rather than leaving a gap highlight this fact and work to fill it with colleagues • a **collaboratively** created living document which is regularly updated
Meetings	Strategy design team: • Meet with initiative owners and delivery office, where exists, to share details on each initiative, with ample time for those who will need to deliver to ask questions • Many, many meetings with delivery owners and others until the strategy is fully delivered.

THE IMPLEMENTATION PLAN

This implementation plan should divide the work to be done into workstreams. Each initiative forms its own workstream. Details should be provided on each initiative, including how it will be deliver and the milestones for the next quarter.

This is also your final chance to confirm the owner and their resources. Particularly for large initiatives, seek to have some people with their time fully dedicated to the initiative. Evidence suggests that where everyone has responsibilities for both "business as usual" and for the new initiative, the new initiative will hardly ever happen as it is just too easy to be pulled back into the day-to-day. Also, often a different mentality is required to deliver the new versus "business as usual."

There is often a need for functional workstreams such as IT or HR to play a role in several workstreams and it makes most sense to have a functional expert coordinating across these.

Finally, all implementation plans must include workstreams on governance and communications. It should also include quarterly milestones for the year ahead, as per the ITC Corporate plan example on the following pages:

Workstreams		Owner	Role	Links to other initiatives	Comments
1	**Key accounts:** Grow the top 6 accounts not up for renewal before 2019	Raghu Jain	Head of Large Business		Will need to delegate targets to account directors; supported by Saffron Jones, Sales Executive, Large Business, who was part of design team
2	**Renewals:** win and increase base	Raghu Jain	Head of Large Business		Will need to delegate targets to account directors; supported by Saffron Jones, Sales Executive, Large Business, who was part of design team
3	**Modularized services:** drawn from packaged services and providing flexible à la carte services	Lisa Evereau	Head of Services Business	10. Marketing	Services Design Director will have heavy day-to-day involvement
4	**Webshop:** which is easy to navigate and use	Des. Evans	Head of Product Business	7. IT & 10. Marketing	Needs close liaison with IT Director, who owns IT workstream

	Workstreams	Owner	Role	Links to other initiatives	Comments
5	**Overseas sales teams:** in Canada, Germany, UK, targeting existing customers with operations there	Janet Daley	Account Director	9. HR & 10. Marketing	Janet to be moved off Kirkton and Jameson and aligned to overseas sales initiative full time
6	**New contracts:** win 3 of cumulatively, at least $75m and $2m profit per year	Kevin Arkwright	Business Development Director		Can build on existing work in business development
7	**IT:** to support IT requirements for initiatives; to ensure IT plans are aligned with strategy	Shelly Jonah	IT Director	4. Webshop	Will need to work in partnership with Head of Product Business to deliver webshop
8	**Finance:** ensure budget plans aligned with strategy; support initiative as required	Irene Andrews	Financial Controller		
9	**HR:** support recruitment of staff, especially for overseas sales initiatives; drive updating of staff's objectives to align with strategy	Jerome Delay	HR Director	5. Overseas sales team	

	Workstreams	Owner	Role	Links to other initiatives	Comments
10	**Marketing:** support development of material and pricing for modularized services, support design of webshop and support design of marketing collateral for overseas teams	Simon Burrows	Marketing Director	3. Modularized services, 4. Webshop & 5. Overseas sales team	
11	**Governance:** Create mechanisms and procedures to share learnings and best practices and monitor performance	James Edwards	Delivery Director		Newly created role, James promoted into this from commercial manager and was part of design team
12	**Communication:** develop ongoing approach and facilitate delivery	Tim Hardy	Communications Director		

For each initiative, recap the proposed approach—as per the detail in the strategy document—and provide detail on finances, as per the example for workstream 5, Overseas sales team below:

Overseas sales team: cost projections

$ 000k	2016			2017		2018	
	Cost per FTE/ item	No of FTEs/ item	Total	Cost per FTE/ item	No of FTEs/ item	Cost per FTE/ item	No of FTEs/ item
CEO	250	1	250	1	250	1	250
Sales staff	120	6	720	10	1200	12	1440
Admin	75	4	300	8	600	9	675
Travel and Expenses	250	1	250	2	500	2.2	550
Office	150	1	150	2	300	2.2	330
IT	50	1	50	2	100	2.2	110
Total costs			1720		2950		3355

Consideration should be given to aligning existing budgets, plans and individuals' objectives with the strategy, tasks that should be undertaken by the associated functional workstream:

- **Alignment with budget:** With your strategy and its expected financial impact and required investment agreed, you want to make sure that all this is reflected in the budget.
  - According to Strategic Planning Toolkit for Dummies[14], 60% of organizations do not link their strategy to budget.
  - Check that yours does and if it does not, detail what needs to happen to address this, including what new revenue and cost lines need to be added and what needs to be removed as no longer part of the strategy
  - Reissue as soon as strategy finalized and certainly within a matter of weeks

- **Alignment of objectives:** Make any changes to objectives and bonus criteria of the division, of teams and individuals to bring these into alignment with the strategy
  - Once you have the initiative owner in place, each needs to review the objectives of their team/the people they are working with to ensure they reflect the strategy
  - All business unit heads need to review the objectives of all their staff to, firstly, make sure that other initiatives that are not part of strategy are not included (and if they are remove them) and, secondly, where appropriate, add new objectives related to the strategy
- **Alignment of IT/other plans:** Ensuring any IT development or other requirements for strategy are appropriately prioritized in plans.

The governance workstream should include the process, metrics, meetings and committees that will be used to share results of pilots (good and bad), facilitate best practice, review performance and support revisions to plans. It also needs to facilitate a can-do culture for delivering the strategy.

The communications workstream should identify the different audiences to communicate with, the frequency and type of message. This workstream will need to be updated as you learn more and circumstances and needs evolve. A thought-through plan at the outset will provide a solid foundation on which to respond flexibly and nimbly.

DELIVERY OFFICE

The delivery office — should you have one — presides over the governance of the program. It acts as the lynchpin coordinating across workstreams and can provide an adjudication role in the instance of disputes. It can also facilitate progress or changing of plans on workstreams to get behind.

You may also choose to have a delivery person or team who get quite actively involved in the details of the workstream plans and in shaping these over time.

There are pros and cons to a delivery office with a more interventionist approach. It can add intellectual weight and rigor behind the implementation plans and where delivery office and initiative owners work well together, will lead to a strong plan and likely more effective joint resolution of problems.

However, it will not work well if there is conflict between the delivery office and initiative owners, especially about who is really in charge (the initiative owner) or if the initiative owner does not take responsibility for their workstream and expects the delivery office to do all the work.

All this suggests that anyone in the delivery office needs to be respected, get on well with people, hold their ground when needed and also be willing to compromise.

Whatever you decide works best for your organization, if you have a delivery office, be sure to clearly define its role and remit and the responsibilities and decision rights of its team.

TESING, PILOTING AND ADAPTING

No implementation plan will get everything 100 percent right from the outset so you need to be able to test approaches and adapt plans in light of learnings.

Let's take a couple of examples for ITC:

- Workstream 5: Overseas sales team. Suppose in Germany, we have been struggling for six months to find a head of the business and that despite getting lots of applicants none of them have been suitable. Then the initiative owner could organize a brainstorm with colleagues, including HR and the delivery office, to identify the issue(s) and how to best address these. For example, do the job adverts inaccurately reflect the skills required, is the salary offered too low, is the role not being advertised in the right place or are they simply expecting too much and being too picky, and so on. Once diagnosed, a mitigating action can be decided and acted upon.

- Workstream 4: Webshop. Suppose that a first version of the webshop has been created. This would be a good time to do some user testing to identify any glitches or areas that are difficult to understand and navigate. Watching the customers use the webshop will provide lots of learnings and inform revisions that may otherwise have been missed.

- Workstream 3: Modularized services: Suppose that there are quite different ways to modularize the services, with differing features and therefore prices accordingly. Why not mock up collateral for the different options and test them with customers? Perhaps none of the options you test will turn-out to be optimal but a mix of them will. Some may not work well at all. This is all valuable insight as otherwise we might never have learned this and ultimately potentially committed more time and money to something that would fail.

Essentially, this really is about mindset. It's about being flexible to test things and having a safe environment to share what doesn't work as much as what did. It is also knowing when to stop something when it is not working or being able to identify which parts are working and which are not, so you can improve output by focusing on what works.

KEEPING ON TRACK

You need to hold yourselves to account for delivering the strategy.

The milestones will help you to see if you are on course, as will feedback from customers, staff and colleagues.

You will no doubt experience times that are challenging or where doubts may emerge. If you have strong relationships in the organization, then you can really use these to support you both on problem solving but also in terms of morale and motivation.

As Edison said when referring to genius, but which also works just as well for a strategy process, is that "it's one percent inspiration and 99 percent perspiration."

UPDATING YOUR STRATEGY

However good an idea, it is rarely good forever. That certainly is true with strategy.

The question I often get asked is whether you will need to update the strategy. In general, the answer is no. This is because you have spent a lot of time thinking it through and so unless conditions really change or it turns out that one of the key initiatives just doesn't work at all—in which case you'd likey need a new one to replace it, with your starting point to review the choices you rejected.

As strategy execution expert Jeroen de Flander says—and with the caveats outlined above: "Strategy is thinking about a choice and choosing to stick with your thinking." And what better reward could there be for this than the realization of your strategy.

CHECKLIST FOR DELIVERING YOUR STRATEGY

- The strategy is divided into workstreams and each has an owner
- Each owner is clear on what he/she needs to deliver and feels empowered to do so
- The plan to implement is documented
- The plan includes details, financials and milestones for each initiative and what the initiatives together will deliver
- The implementation plan describes the approach to governance including metrics and committees
- The plan includes the ongoing communication approach.

A FINAL NOTE

WHERE TO GO FROM HERE

Congratulations! You now have a strategy that is actionable, rigorous that has been created collaboratively.

Designing a Strategy that Works has shown you how to articulate your goal, how to choose the options to meet it and how to craft these choices into an integrated strategy that will work. Learning the steps outlined in this book also has benefits far beyond the areas of strategy design and implementation. The techniques in each of the chapters are standalone—for example, the techniques on structuring thinking and on the Minto Pyramid Principle® can transform verbal and written communications, from a short email to a more formal presentation. Or take the ability to accurately frame a problem: I just think how often with clear framing misunderstanding and heartache could be avoided.

Yet we all know that your strategy is not worth the paper it is written on if it remains undelivered. So from here your focus is execution, execution, execution!

Write down in the space provided overleaf three action items you commit to taking over the next 45 days. For example, you may want to do a one day offsite implementation planning session, or perhaps you need to determine the governance structure for the implementation phase.

1. _____
   _____
   _____
   _____
   _____

2. _____
   _____
   _____
   _____
   _____

3. _____
   _____
   _____
   _____

Take every opportunity to use and practice the techniques in this book. If you apply these techniques and insights, you will create a successful strategy and see impact well beyond that.

I would be delighted to hear from you with your feedback on the approach in this book. So please do get in touch with your comments at sarahthrift@insightconsults.com.

May your strategy be realized and every success yours,

APPENDIX

Commentary and answers to exercises in the book.

CHAPTER 2:

IDENTIFYING WHICH QUESTIONS ARE SMART ONES

Questions 1 to 3:

Answer Yes / No	1. What makes ITC profitable?	2. Can ITC double its business?	3. What organizational changes are required for ITC to double its business?
Specific	Y	N	Y
Measurable	N	Y	Y
Actionable	N	N	Y
Relevant	Y	Y	N
Time-bound	N	N	N
Open	Y	N	Y
Non-assumptive	Y	Y	N
Expansive	Y	Y	Y

Comments:

1. What makes ITC profitable?

   - This will provide an answer that is quite narrow—almost like a yes/no question—and also one that refers to profitability today. This is not necessarily an indicator of profitability in the future and hardly the basis for a robust strategy.

2. Can ITC double its business?

   - Closed question (yes/no answer) without revealing the reasoning behind the answer and if yes, the actions that could be taken to deliver it.

3. What organizational changes are required for ITC to double its business?

   - Assumptive question. Unless a lot of prior work has already been done and has clearly revealed that organizational changes are what is needed, starting off with this question makes it likely you will fail to notice other solutions that would have much greater impact. Whenever I am contacted to help with determining organizational changes, a red flag immediately pops up in my head: organizational changes are very disruptive. This does not mean of course that they should never be undertaken, however they need to emerge as part of a broader strategy and not as *the* strategy itself.

Questions 4 to 6:

Answer Yes / No	4. How can ITC add 50% to its revenue in the next two years, while at least maintaining current profit margins?	5. Create a proposition to generate significant and sustainable return for ITC and the customer	6. In what ways can ITC add 50% to its profitability while maintaining customer satisfaction scores?
Specific	Y	Y	Y
Measurable	Y	N	Y
Actionable	Y	Y	Y
Relevant	Y	N	N
Time-bound	Y	N	N
Open	Y	Y	Y
Non-assumptive	Y	Y	N
Expansive	Y	N	Y

4. How can ITC add 50% to its revenue in the next two years, while at least maintaining current profit margins?

- This is the most suitable question so far. It is effectively talking about at least doubling profitability—which we know the CEO thinks is possible. My two further questions would be (a) while we want a stretching goal, is this achievable? Only the CEO seems to think this is possible and none of the rest of the leadership team and (b) is two years a sufficient timeframe? As a general rule, three years is the most common timeframe for a strategy. Beyond that, and certainly beyond five years really is too uncertain to design for with any precision. Two years, by contrast, can be a bit short-term in focus.

5. Create a proposition to generate significant and sustainable return for ITC and the customer

   • Stating the obvious, but this is not a question.

6. In what ways can ITC add 50% to its profitability while maintaining customer satisfaction scores?

   • Unclear if the criteria specified on customer satisfaction is important or not. If it were, we may expect it to be listed in the context about ITC in Chapter 1.

CHAPTER 4:

WHAT YOU SEE IS ALL THERE IS

Answer: Many people answer that the bat is $1. If this is the case, the ball must be $0.10 and so the bat is only $0.90 more than the ball. The correct answer is bat $1.05 and ball $0. 05.

OVERCONFIDENCE BIAS

To estimate, all for 2015	Actual
1. GDP per capita in the US	$54,577
2. Proportion of books sold in electronic format in the US	20%
3. Proportion of American public school students qualifying for free or reduced school lunches	51%
4. Population of European Union	508m
5. Number of nations in the United Nations	193
6. Your organization's worldwide revenue 2015	For you to check (and not simply guess)
7. Your organization's worldwide net assets, 31 December 2015	For you to check (and not simply guess)
8. Your organization's worldwide employee turnover 2015 (%)	For you to check (and not simply guess)

CHAPTER 5:

SPECIFIC, MEANINGFUL AND TESTABLE HYPOTHESES

Below are comments on the example hypotheses in Chapter 5:

- Our customers can be segmented
  - This is neither specific nor meaningful. Pretty much all sets of customers can be segmented. The important point—which is not in the question—is how they can be segmented and what insight would this provide if you were to do so.

- We should focus on customers who are looking for a low cost offering to improve their profitability
  - This is meaningful and testable, and somewhat specific, as it tells us where to focus. I would also want to know with this hypothesis or any similar ones, what this low cost offering would be.

- Our primary customer base needs a high-quality, efficient service and is prepared to pay a premium for this
  - This is specific, meaningful and testable. You would need to talk to customers to test it, but it is specific enough to check there is a need for this.

- Revenue growth is important to restore ITC's profitability
  - This is easily testable, but falls short in terms of being meaningful and specific. For example, I'd like to know how important revenue is to meeting the $50m profit target. For example is it 90% of the answer or 50%?—"important" in this context could mean either.

ACKNOWLEDGMENTS

The author would like to thank the following people for their support and contributions in making this book happen:

Irian Christine Weber, who has been an invaluable support to me as a friend and colleague since 2007. I am not quite sure where to start with the thanks ... editor extraordinaire, thinking partner, problem solver, late night and early morning ear ... and much more. Neither my business nor my book would be what it is without her. Thank you.

Nicole Sultana, who has been the ever present thought partner and editor on this third edition and who has brought great skill in ensuring the translation of ideas into precise techniques and actions as part of this book.

Tanicia Baynes, founder of Lollifox Design Studio, who is the designer of this and other Insight publications. As you are experiencing, Tanicia brings beautiful, clear and sharp design, helping the words to spring from the page.

Emma Vuletic, who edited the early chapters of this book and who adds lightness and clarity with her words.

To DrAfter123 whom I have never had the pleasure to meet and who designed the wonderful images for this book.

Amy Celento who made herself and her home available for me to write. Amy, thank you for your wisdom and generosity—and your kitchen table.

Neil Almond, without whom none of this might ever have happened. He started it all, as I stood in his offices at a flip-chart, with the question: "If I could get a group of CEOs together, could you teach us what you do?"

Aliceson Robinson, a wonderful teacher, coach and workshop leader from whom I have learned a lot through the strategy courses we taught together.

Paolo Cuomo for his support and his feedback following detailed reads of the book.

Raj Modi, of www.strategyexpert.com who encouraged my writings and gave me invaluable feedback as a course participant.

My friend Katerina Zographos for her support and wisdom.

My friends, colleagues and clients from McKinsey & Company who taught me so much and set high expectations for me to always aim for.

All the members of the Insight team over the years for their support and feedback that helped evolve the business and its services.

My clients and course participants—I have so enjoyed working alongside you, teaching you and learning with you.

And to Dr. Mohan Kataria, who is sadly no longer with us, but whose love and inspiration I will treasure forever.

NOTES

Introduction:

1. Research conducted by William Schiemann as published in *Performance Management: Putting Research into Action.*

2. Economist Intelligence Unit, *Why good strategies fail: lessons from the C-Suite,* July 2013.

Chapter 1:

3. Michael Porter quote, as published in *Harvard Business Review: What Is Strategy?,* November – December 1996.

Chapter 4:

4. Kahneman, D; Tversky, A. (1973) Judgement Under Uncertainty: Heuristics and Biases.

5. A film called *Moneyball* starring Brad Pitt and Jonah Hill based on the book *Moneyball: The art of Winning an Unfair Game* by Michael Lewis was released in 2011.

6. Kahneman, D, *Thinking Fast and Slow,* (New York: Farrar, Straus and Giroux, 2013).

7. Alpert, Marc; Raiffa, Howard (1982)." A progress report on the training of probability assessors", in *Judgment under uncertainty: Heuristics and Biases,* edited by Daniel Kahneman, Paul Slovic, and Amos Tversky.

8. McKenzie, C.R.M., Liersch, M. J., & Yaniv, I (2008). "Overconfidence in interval estimates: What does expertise buy you?" in *Organizational Behavior and Human Decision Processes,* Vol. 107, pp179—91.

9. Ben Saunders, "Opt-out organ donation without presumptions" Journal of Medical Ethics, Vol. 38: 69-72 (2012); (http://jme.bmj.com/content/38/2/69).

10. You may also see a PEST analysis talked about. This is the same concept, less the Legal and Environmental components.

11. Minto, B. (2002), *The Pyramid Principle*, (London: Pearson Edition)

12. It is no coincidence that the pyramid, turned by 90 degrees, looks just like our question tree earlier. The same general principle—a governing thought or question supported by logically grouped findings or sub-questions—applies. However, the pyramid can be, but does not need to be MECE—one fact, a change in regulation for example, can support a number of ideas higher up in the pyramid or later when we use the pyramid to structure our choices, which by definition are not collectively exhaustive.

Chapter 8:

13. These first four enablers are part of the McKinsey 7S, which also includes strategy, style and shared values.

Chapter 10:

14. Olsen, E (2011). *Strategic Planning Kit for Dummies*, (For Dummies)

BIBLIOGRAPHY

Alpert, Marc; Raiffa, Howard. (1982), A progress report on the training of probability assessors", in *Judgment under uncertainty: Heuristics and Biases*. Cambridge University Press.

Bazerman, M.H. and Moore, D.A. (2013), Judgment in Managerial Decision Making, 8th Edition, New York: Wiley & Sons

Bazerman, M.H. (2014), The Power of Noticing, 1st Edition, New York: Simon and Schuster

Collins, T. (2009), Change by Design, New York: Harper Collins

Friga, P.N. (2009), The McKinsey Engagement, New York: McGraw-Hill

Gelb, M.J.(1998), How to Think Like Leonardo Da Vinci, New York: Random House

Heath, C. & Heath, D. (2013), Decisive: How to Make Better Choices in Life and Work, New York: Crown Publishing Group

Kahneman, D. (2013), Thinking Fast and Slow, New York: Farrar, Straus and Giroux, 2013

Kahneman, D. Slovic, P; Tversky, A. (1982), Judgment Under Uncertainty: Heuristics and Biases, Cambridge: Cambridge University Press

McKenzie, C.R.M., Liersch, M. J., & Yaniv, I.(2008), "Overconfidence in interval estimates: What does expertise buy you?" in *Organizational Behavior and Human Decision Processes*, Vol. 107.

Minto, B. (2002), The Pyramid Principle, London: Pearson Education

Raisel, E.M. (1998), The McKinsey Way, New York: McGraw-Hill

Raisel, E.M. & Friga, P.N. (2001), The McKinsey Mind, New York: McGraw-Hill

Rosser, B. (2009), Better, Stronger, Faster: Build it, Scale it, Flog it—The Entrepreneur's Guide to Success in Business, Oxford Infinite Ideas Limited

Zelazny, G. (1985), Say it with Charts, New York: McGraw-Hill

INDEX

ABOUT INSIGHT CONSULTANCY SOLUTIONS

Insight Consultancy Solutions is a boutique consultancy and training company founded in 2007, with offices in the US and UK.

Insight delivers projects in strategy design, development and implementation, and provides expertise in multiple sectors including technology, financial services, education, public policy and NGOs.

A specialty of Insight is the design and facilitation of strategic problem-solving and communication courses for organizations, entrepreneurs and consultants. These courses are led by Sarah Thrift and her team of highly experienced consultants, who have spent thousands of hours using these tools and techniques in their own consulting work, in addition to the hundreds of hours they have spent teaching the material.

ABOUT THE AUTHOR

Sarah Thrift has 16 years experience working with businesses and nonprofit organizations on strategy, leadership and change management.

Prior to founding Insight Consultancy Solutions, Sarah worked at McKinsey & Company and as a policy advisor on business at the UK Treasury led by Gordon Brown, UK Chancellor and subsequently Prime Minister.

Sarah's mission is to pass her expertise and knowledge on strategic thinking, problem solving and decision-making to her clients. She teaches highly sought-after courses in these areas and shares the essence of her skills with those she cannot work with directly through her writing.

Sarah has a Masters in math from Imperial College, London where she received the Governors' prize for achieving the top first class honors of her class. She has a great love of learning and has completed many courses since, including at Oxford University and Harvard University.